SUSSEX COUNTY DELAWARE

WILL BOOK L:
1 JANUARY 1852 - 24 FEBRUARY 1860

ABSTRACTED BY

MARGUERITE R. MOORE

HERITAGE BOOKS
2007

HERITAGE BOOKS
AN IMPRINT OF HERITAGE BOOKS, INC.

Books, Cds, and more—Worldwide

For our listing of thousands of titles see our website
at
www.Heritagebooks.com

Published 2007 by
HERITAGE BOOKS, INC.
Publishing Division
65 East Main Street
Westminster, Maryland 21157-5026

International Standard Book Number: 978-1-58549-336-4

Special thanks to my husband
FRED A. MOORE
for his encouragement and computer skills

Dedicated to his Grandmother
SARAH ELIZABETH MARVEL
1849-1929

The search for her Delaware ancestors
was the inspiration for this book

Marguerite R. Moore
7730 Emerson Ave
Los Angeles, CA 90045-1117

fredmo@ix.netcom.com

Abbreviations

Bond: surety at probate

EX-ref: named as executor but refused to serve

Land: Property sold to, bought from, adjacent to, location, etc.

Mentioned (Men): no relationship stated

SUSSEX CO DELAWARE WILLS

BOOK L

pg 1
LINGO, Jesse   13NOV1851   1JAN1852
Son: Mires B. (EX). Daus: Louisa H., Sarah A., Hetty R. Wit: Isaac WAPLES, T. W. BURTON.

pg 2
DULANY, Levin W.   NWF H.   19DEC1851   13JAN1852
Wife: Martha Elizabeth. Son: James Henry. Dau: Mary Elenor. Bro: William W. (EX). Sis: Eunice ROSS. Men: Meshack ELLIOTT. William H. ROSS (EX). Wit:Majer W. ALLEN, Joseph P.H. SHIPLEY, William E. ROGERS.

pg 5
CLENDANIEL, George Sr   Cedar Cr H.   14DEC1851   13JAN1852
Wife: Gemima. Sons: George, John (EX). Grsons: William STAPLEFORD, Nathaniel STAPLEFORD, John CLENDANIEL, Samuel H. CLENDANIEL, John Harlan CLENDANIEL (son/ Benjamin (dec)); John CLENDANIEL & Benjamin CLENDANIEL (sons/ George). Grdaus: Sally TOWNSEND (wife/ David), Elizabeth PIERCE (wife/ John), Sarah Catherine CLENDANIEL, Sally CLENDANIEL (dau/ George). Men: James RICKARDS (grson/ Gemima CLENDANIEL). Clement H. HUDSON (EX). Land: James RICKARDS (dec), John TOWNSEND. Wit: Lemuel B. STOCKLEY, Spicer WARREN, Nancy Ann WARREN.

pg 7
PHILLIPS, Spencer   Dags. H.   17OCT1851   13JAN1852
Wife: Eunice A. Sons: John R., Elihu G., Joshua (EX), Nathaniel. Daus: Eunice Jane RICKARDS, Sarah A. MELSON, Levinia OTWELL, Mary Ann TRUITT. Grsons: Spencer A. PHILLIPS, Greensbury T. PHILLIPS (son/ Elihu). Grdau: Sarah E. PHILLIPS (dau/ Elihu). Bro: Shepherd. Wit: James B. BLIZZARD, James TRUITT, John K. TRUITT.

pg 10
ELZEY, Robert   Little Cr H.   16DEC1851   13JAN1852
Wife: Mary (EX). Son: Alfred. Bros: Arnold, Charles. Sis: Elizabeth ELLIS. Men: Rachel PHILLIPS (wife/ Noah). EX- Nathaniel HORSEY. Wit: Stephen GREEN, Andrew S. PUSEY, C. C. WINDSOR.

pg 12
WILLIS, Fisher H.   Nanticoke H.   26MAY1851   23FEB1852
Half-bro: Luther M. WELCH. Half-sis: Amelia F. WELCH, Janney G. WELCH, Margaret J. WELCH (EX), Sarah F. SHARP. Niece: Sarah Ann WELCH (dau/ half-bro George A. WELCH). Wit: W.W. STUART, Joseph O. WELCH.

pg 14
JONES, William   Worcester Co MD   6MAY1845   5OCT1845
Son: William Bishop (EX). Dau: Polly. Sis: Sally PARSONS (wife/ John A.). Nephews: James Asbury PARSONS, William PARSONS, John Burton PARSONS (sons/ Sally). Niece: Nancy Elizabeth PARSONS (dau/ Sally). Wit: Samuel MELSON, Nathaniel R. VINSON, Elijah M. BRITTINGHAM.

pg 16
CORDREY, Spencer   16SEP1849   19MAR1852
Sons: William B. (EX), Spencer M. Grdaus: Mary M. HENRY (wife/ Luther), Hessy A. CORDREY, Jane HENRY (wife/ C. W.), Polly P. SMITH (wife/ John William). Wit: Doughty COLLINS, Thomas W. RECORDS.

pg 18
BLADES, Mary   Seaford   12AUG1851   18MAY1852
Sons: James Madison, William (EX). Daus: Lavinia WILLIAMS (wife/ John),
    Rebecca COLLISON (wife/ William). Land: Daniel CANNON. Wit: Louder CANNON, J.J. JENKINS.

1

WAPLES, Cornelius   Ind Riv H.   7JUL1852   27JUL1852
Wife: Jane. Sons: Cornelius, Joseph Henry, James Edward, Benton Marvel, David Mustard, Alfred. Sons: Sharon,
John, George (EX), (sons/ 1st wife). Daus: Eliza ALLEN, Mary Ellinor VICKERS (?). Land: Dags. H. Wit: John
MARTIN, William N. THOROUGHGOOD.

JAMES, Caldwell W.   planter   11MAR1850   20JUL1852
Wife: Mary (EX). Sons: Branson D. (EX), Erais Thomas, Noah H., John Edward. Daus: Elenah A. SHORT, Leah
A., Mary E. Land: John SHORT, William JAMES, Neolden TINDLE, Miles TINDLE. Wit: John ROGERS,
Curtis A. CONNAWAY, Selby CONNAWAY.

BRERETON,, Sarah   Milton   6MAR1852   JUL1852
Grson: David R. COOPER (EX). EX-John PONDER Wit: Charles MANSHIP, James PONDER.
TOWNSEND, Moses   colored man Little Cr H.   14JUL1851   7SEP1852
Wife: Rachal. Son: Allen. Bros: Cutter, Peter BOYCE (have ch). Land: William DULANEY, Cyrus C.
WINDSOR, Joseph SMITH. Wit: Joseph SMITH, Charles C. SANDERS.

DONOVAN, Mary   Broadkiln H.   8JUL1848   15OCT1852
Sons: Abraham, Kendal (EX). Dau: Elizabeth MESSICK (wife/ William). Wit: William A. HAZZARD. William
W. WOLFE.

DAVIS, William   Broadkiln H.   13AUG1852   15OCT1852
Wife: unnamed. Sons: William, Charles. Dau: Mary STUART (wife/ John). EX- Thomas A. MOORE.
Wit:JohnPONDER, John TILNEY.

TURNER, Daniel   Nanticoke H.   31OCT1852   11NOV1852
Sons: Charles H. , Isaac E. (both U21). "All my children". Mentioned: Torbert TURNER (U21). Leah M.
TURNER, Noah VINCENT, Miles SANDERS. EX- Alexander FISHER. Wit: Minos T. CONNAWAY, John D.
SEAVIN.

STEEL, James   Broadkiln H.   27APR1852   17NOV1852
Wife: Penelope K. (EX). Sons: James M., John C., William T., George M. (sons/ Penelope). Dau: Eliza F. (dau/
Penelope). Daus: Mary E. & Maria F. HUNTER (wife/ Albert) (daus/ 1st wife, Maria FISHER). Ch: Ishmael (EX),
Hester E. CARY (wife/ Albert), Sarah Ann (ch/ 2nd wife, Ann WALTON). Land: Mary R. HARRIS
(Georgetown), Jonathan SHOEMAKER, Priscilla REYNOLDS, Adolphus P. EWING. Wit: John R. MC FEE.
John B. WAPLES, Kendal B. WINGATE.

GOSLEN, Hester   13NOV1852   23NOV1852
Daus: Ann Eliza, Mary Catherine, Sarah Emma, Hester Lavinia (all U21). Ex- John KINDER & Nathaniel
HORSEY. Wit: John R. SUDLER, George P. WHITE.

JOHNSON, Burton   tanner Ind Riv H.   4DEC1852   16DEC1852
Sons: James H, Burton, Robert W. Daus: Elizabeth WILLIAMS, Patience STREET, Mary PARKINSON. Grson:
Eben Leonard. Grdaus: Mary (dau/ Elizabeth), Mary (dau/ Mitchel) (both U21). Son-law: Harma PARKINSON.
EX- Levin SOCKUM. Wit: James P. WALLS, James B. COFFIN, Arcada G. COFFIN.

pg 43

EVANS, Zadoc   5FEB1848   20DEC1852
Wife: Nancy. Sons: John, Clement, Henry, Jacob, William T. Daus: Rhoda, Elizabeth D. LINCH, Nancy BENNETT. Grsons: unnamed (son/ John W. EVANS), Zadoc Aydelotte. Wit: William S. HALE, Isaiah ELLIS, Henry J. HALL.

pg 45

WALLS, William (son/ Peter)   16FEB1852   14DEC1852
Wife: Izabel (EX). Son: Jonathan W. Daus: Eliza Ann, Emely W. Wit: Hugh C. COY, Nathaniel W. BURTON. Cod: 26NOV1852 Wit: Levin W. WAPLES, James A. COFFIN.

pg 47

WILSON, James   22AUG1840   23DEC1852
Sons: Zacheriah (EX), William W. (EX), Harry. Daus: Mary HANDREACK (has son Kendal), Elizabeth DUTTON (has dau Elizabeth), Charlotte. Land: Jonathan DICKERSON, Jonathan SHOEMAKER, James ROUSE, Peter ROBINSON, Daniel JESTER. Wit: James A. PARKER, Peter S. PARKER.

pg 50

MORRIS, Stephen   farmer Dags. H.   10DEC1852   20JAN1853
Sons: Stephen C. (dec), James (dec). Dau: Nancy A. MARVEL (EX), Grsons: David M., George F., Joseph B. (sons/ Stephen C.). Grdau: Penelope K. WARREN. Land: Robert JEFFERSON, Joseph B. MORRIS, Robert WARREN, Bethesda Meeting House. Wit: William ANDERSON, Hiram JOHNSON.

pg 52

BARR, Robert   Nanticoke H.   15MAR1844   27JAN1853
Wife: Betsey (EX). Sons: David W. (EX), Robert P., James R. (of MO). Daus: Hetty SPICER (wife/ James (of MO), Eliza MC CAULLY (wife/ Peter P.), Lovey H., Nancy CONNAWAY (dec), Mary R. KNOWLES (wife/ Daniel). Grdau: Elizabeth CONNAWAY (dau/ Nancy). Land: Cornelius PRETTYMAN, Nathaniel P. HARRIS, William JONES (dec). Wit: Cyrus Q. FOOKS, George FRAME.

pg 54

PARKER, Peter Sr   Milton   20SEP1852   31JAN1853
Wife: unnamed (dec). Sons: Peter C. (EX), John R., Samuel P., William R., Theodore S. Dau: Mary WELCH (wife/ Nehemiah D.) Grsons: George WELCH (son/ Nehemiah D.), illegible, Peter Parker WELCH (son/ Nehemiah D.). Wit: Robert M. HALL, John C. HAZZARD.

pg 57

LYNCH, Gilbert   Baltimore H.   14NOV1850   15MAR1853
Wife: Elizabeth. Sons: Isaiah, Aaron, Alfred. Dau: Nancy (U21). Grdau: Willmena CARLENE (U21). Land: Little BASCON, N. Evans RICKARDS (dec). Wit: N.W. EVANS, James LYNCH, Rheuben LYNCH.

pg 58

CAMPBELL, John   24FEB1853   17MAR1853
Wife: Mary. Son: Robert S. Daus: Hannah BUCHANAN (wife/ James), Mary HUDSON (wife/ John), Catherine, Susan J., Elizabeth L., Charlotte S. Grdaus: Mary C. & Anna C. BUCHANAN (daus/ Hannah & James). Wit: Purnal T. BENNETT, David H. HOLLAND. Joseph ARGOE.

pg 61

DAWSON, Prudence   NWF H.   11NOV1841   22MAR1853
Dau: Sarah Jane. EX-ref: William ANDERSON (/Kent Co DE). Wit: William M. SIMPSON, William B. SIMPSON, John HICKMAN.

pg 63

WEST, James   11DEC1849   29MAR1853
Wife: Peggy. Father: Jehu. Son: John C. (EX). Daus: Nancy SHORT, Mary JONES. Grsons: James A., William J., James H. JONES. Grdau: Margaret Ann JONES. Land: Manuel VINSON (negro). Wit: Jacob WOOTTEN, Philip TRUITT, Margaret Ann HEARN.

3

pg 65
MARVEL, Philip   Dags. H.   16MAR1853   4APR1853
Wife: Elizabeth M.   Sons: Philip Rodney (EX), George Edward (EX).   Apprentice: William TIMMONS.   Wit:
Nutter MARVEL, John WAPLES.

pg 67
O'NEAL, Josiah   Broad Cr. H.   29MAR1852   5APR1853
Wife: Abigal.   Sons: Thomas, William (EX), Cyrus, Anthony.   Daus: Peggy WARD, Mary OWENS.   Grson:
William CHIPMAN (U21).   "All my grandchildren" Land: Peggy ELLEGOOD (dec), Little Creek H., Henry
BENSON.   Wit: Joseph W. BACON, John MOORE, C.C. WINDSOR.

pg 70
EDGIN, Mary   NWF H.   26FEB1850   12APR1853
Sons: William (EX), Robert.   Daus: Milley, Jane, Sarah KNOWLES, Luisa CUBBAGE.   Wit: Wesley SMITH,
Samuel CUBBAGE, Millie EDGIN.

pg 71
WARRINGTON, James D.   Ind Riv H.   21JUL1852   13APR1853
Wife: Elizabeth B. (EX).   Sons: John Wesley, James Henry (both U21).   Dau: Sarah Ann (U21).   Wit: James F.
BURTON, Elizabeth JOSEPH.

pg 73
POLK, Josiah   Cedar Cr H.   9MAR1853   12APR1853
Sis: Sarah Lofland POLK, Jenetty PRATT (has ch).   Nephew: William J. POLK .EX-ref: William PORTER.   Wit:
Manlove JOHNSON, Mark Greer LOFLAND.

pg 75
WATSON, Priscilla   Lewes   24MAR1851   12APR1853
Sons: William, Edward (EX).   Daus: Susan SMALLWOOD, Ann BRICK, Julia Ann BARROWS.   Grdau: Mary
SMALLWOOD.   Wit: D.B. TINKER, Joseph LAFETRA.

pg 76
RILEY, Betsey   28MAR1850   5MAY1853
Mentioned: Sina WARREN (wife/ John), Robert L. Harris WARREN (son/ John), Sally Ann Talbert
CARPENTER (widow, EX).   Alexander WARREN (son/ John), Stephen WARREN (son/ S.) EX.   Wit: Isaac F.
WARREN, William WARREN.

pg 78
LEWIS, Stephen   Dags H.   1NOV1849   24MAY1853
Son: Joseph (EX).   Daus: Rachel STONE (wife/ John), Nancy LONG (wife/ David).   Wit: Thomas LOWE, Jacob
GUNBY, Thomas MITCHELL.

pg 79
MESSICK, Nathan   Broad Cr H.   6MAR1847   6JUN1853
Wife: Salley.   Sons: Claton C., William W. (EX), Selby C.   Land: John MESSICK (son/ I), Joel MESSICK.   Wit:
Eli G. SMITH, John MESSICK, John W. MESSICK.

pg 81
PRETTYMAN, Shepard   28FEB1846   6JUN1853
Sons: William (EX), Isaac.   Dau: Lydia Milby CARY (wife/ John).   Wit: Barkley WILSON, James WALLS (son/
P.).

FOOKS, Thomas Sr. Merchant Broad Cr. H 19MAY1848 26JUL1853
Wife: Sally. Sons: Isaac N. (EX), Thomas H. (EX). Daus: Lavinia COTTINGHAM (wife/ Alfred), Elizabeth
WILSON (wife/ David M.), Mary JAMES (wife/ Hiram H.), Gincy BACON (widow/ Jonathan), Priscilla. Grson:
John R. WILSON. Land:John TINDAL (son/ P.) of Nanticoke H., Concord. Wit: Caleb S. LAYTON, Caleb R.
LAYTON.

COLLINS, Rev. Levin A. 13APR1853 27JUL1853
Wife: Julia A. (EX). Daus: Georgia Anna, Isadorah Emely, Julia Eva. Bro-law: Rev. Thomas A. MOORE (EX).
Men: Methodist Church. Wit: William W. DASHIELLS, Thomas J. SAUNDERS.

SWEENY, John Lewes 11JUN1853 6AUG1853
Sons: John, Edward, Charles, Arthur W. Daus: Mary C., Elizabeth. EX- Henry WOLFE. Land: Joshua S.
BENTON. . Wit: George CHAMBERS, William M. FOWLER.

SHARP, Emely (Amelia) Broadkiln H. 29JUN1853 15AUG1853
Sons: Nathaniel Starr (EX), Henry. Father-law: Jacob. Wit: William W. WOLFE, D.E. WOLFE.

STEEN, Curtis 5APR1849 16AUG1853
Wife: Lavenia. Sons: Thomas, James, Ephraim (EX-ref). Daus: Mary SCOTT (dec), Hetty Ann SHORT, Eliza
RICKARDS, Sarah Insley, Nancy. Grson: William (son/ Nancy). EX-ref: Caleb S. LAYTON. Land: James
WEBB (dec).Wit: Robert A. HOUSTON, Caleb Rodney LAYTON. Cod: 26OCT1852 Son: Ephraim. Grson:
James SCOTT (son/ Mary). Grdau: Naomi S. SCOTT. Mentioned: Levin STEEN (son/ Thomas). Wit: Robert A.
HOUSTON.

HOLLAND, Elijah 5AUG1853 23AUG1853
Wife: Mary (heir/ John HOOD). Land: William P. ORR. Wit: H.F. HALL, Thomas WALKER.

RODNEY, Daniel (son/ William) Broad Cr H. 20MAR1838 27SEP1853
Sons: Robert M. (EX), John. Daus: Nancy, Betsey, Mary, Sarah. Land: Nehemiah REDDEN (Adm/ John
MELSON), Laurel. Wit: George R. FISHER, John P. BRINKLOE.

NEAL, William NWF H. 22AUG1853 29SEP1853
Wife: Mary Ann. Sons: William (EX), Isaiah (dec) (has 2ch U21), Arthur (EX). Daus: Mary Jane ANDER (wife/
Ager), Elizabeth CONAWAY (dec) (wife/ William P.) Grson: William Charles (U21) (son/ James). Note: Winder
DASHIELL (dec). Wit: Thomas JACOBS, Nathaniel HORSEY, William W. SPICER.

REYNOLDS, Priscilla 10AUG1847 10OCT1853
Daus: Mary ROBBINS (wife/ Joseph (EX)), Betsey TAYLOR (wife/ David). Grson: David M. REYNOLDS. Wit:
John SHARP, Asa SHARP, James STEEL.

DAZEY, Matilda 9JUL1851 22OCT1853
Sons: Jacob, Richard. Daus: Julia A. WHARTON, Elizabeth B. TONAEUS (?), Susan (EX). Grson: Walter S.
DAZEY. Wit: Walter E. JEFFERSON, Henry HUDSON.

pg 107
WAPLES, Isaac   4JAN1853   24OCT1853
Wife: Mary Ann. Son: William D. (EX). Dau: Letty STOCKLEY (wife/ Kendal B.). Men: Susan HURT. Wit: William N. THOROUGHGOOD, John BURTON.

pg 109
WILLEY, Nehemiah   NWF H.   18FEB1853   22NOV1853
Wife: Susan (EX). "All my ch" (all U21). EX- John WILLEY. Wit: Garret S. LAYTON, James CANNON, William CANNON

pg 110
BENNETT, Jehu   Baltimore H.   30NOV1849   28NOV1853
Wife: Nancy. Sons: James, Nathaniel (dec). Grsons: Jehu, Levin H.E. (son/ James), Samuel D. (EX), Charles D., John S., John (son/ James) (hus/ Elizabeth), Joshua R. (son/ Nathaniel). Grdaus: Maria RICKARDS (wife/ Isaac), Mary DERICKSON, Rhoda Elizabeth (dau/ James), Rachel R. (dau/ Nathaniel), Emeline R. GRAY (dau/ Nathaniel BENNETT), Ann W. (dau/ Nathaniel), Mary Ann. Mentioned: Nancy W. TAYLOR (dau/ Betsey WILLGEN), Mary Ann TAYLOR. Land: Nathaniel DERICKSON, John DERICKSON, Jehu DERICKSON, Benjamin HUDSON, Jehu CLAY (?)(dec), William RICKARDS (dec), Burton R. TUBBS, Levin H. DERICKSON, Elijah EVANS, Kendal RICKARDS, James MILLER. Wit: Peleg W. HELMS, Charles TAYLOR, George L. MORRIS, Rachel JUSTICE.

pg 114
DRAPER, Thomas Sr.   Cedar Cr H.   12AUG1845   5DEC1853
Sons: Thomas Jr (EX), Miers C. (EX), Henry. Dau: Elizabeth. Grdau: Josephine (U21). Mentioned: James W. DRAPER. Wit: Joshua G. BAKER, Sarah C. BAKER, Jacob W. WEBB.

pg 117
KNOWLES, Daniel   Nanticoke H.   15FEB1851   6DEC1853
Wife: Mary R. Sons: Daniel L., William, Robert. Daus: Eliza Jane JAMES, Julia Ann (youngest), Sarah Catherine (youngest), Elizabeth TAYLOR(wife/ James), Mary Ann. Mentioned: Jane KOLLOCK(late wife). Land: Josiah MARVEL, Thomas WILKINS, Isaac WILLEN, Thomas WILLEN, Polly ALLEN, Cyrus FLEETWOOD, Noble CONNAWAY (dec), Robert BARR, Warren PRETTYMAN (dec). Wit: C.B. SEPPLE, Philip C. JONES. Bond: Urias T. JAMES, John WEST.

pg 122
HOBBS, Mary   7SEP1853   8DEC1853
Mentioned: Joseph SULLIVAN (U21), George P. HOBBS (U21), Sarah G. SULLIVAN. Wit: William H. STAFFORD, Elizabeth CANNON.

pg 123
JACOBS, Timothy   free negro   Broadkiln H.   3OCT1853   12DEC1853
Sons: Curtis, Robert, Minos, Noah. Daus: Elizabeth, Mary, Starlina (?). Land: Georgetown, Robert BARR. Dinah WHITE. EX- Joseph B. VAUGHN. Wit: James B. COFFIN, William H. VAUGHAN.

PG 124
DAVIS, Brinkley   Broadkiln H.   11MAY1850   16DEC1853
Wife: Hester Ann. Sons: Nehemiah A., John, Solomon, Henry, Joshua, Brinkley, William R. Daus: Caroline, Hester Ann, Mary SATTERFIELD (widow), Elizabeth INGRAM (wife/ John), Sally CONNAWAY (wife/ John). Grdaus: Sally Ann SATTERFIELD (dau/ Mary), Ellen TINDAL. EX- James REDDEN. Land: Thomas G. WEST (dec). Wit: William W. WOLFE, David E. WOLFE.

pg 126
ARGOE, Abigail   APR1850   27DEC1853
Husband: Alexander. Dau: Nancy DARBY. Grson: Elexander Burton DARBY.. Wit: John CAMPBELL (now dec), Charlotte CAMPBELL. Bond: Nancy M. DARBE, John P. HUDSON.

6

pg 127

TWILLEY, Robert   Little Cr H.   27JAN1851   3JAN1854
Sons: James (EX), Levin P. (EX). Grson: Joseph P. Grdaus: Elenor A. PHILLIPS; Maria M. & Julia (daus/ Levin by 1st wife); Emaline & Mary J. (U18). Land: Jonathan BAILEY, Ebben WALLER. Wit: Samuel KINNEY, Thomas W. RECORDS.

pg 129

MURRAY, David   Baltimore H.   23AUG1853   16JAN1854
Son: Joshua B. (EX). Daus: Hetty S. DAVIS (eldest, widow), Mary MC CABE (wife/ John), Sarah S.(youngest). Wit: Josiah T. SELBY, Jacob HICKMAN, John MELVIN.

pg 131

PAYNTER, John   Lewes & Rehoboth H.   23APR1850   17JAN1854
Son: Joseph R. Daus: Elizabeth (EX), Jane MARSHALL (wife/ Aaron (EX)), Lydia M. WOLFE (wife/ Rice). Mentioned: Samuel R. PAYNTER, Dr. Henry F. HALL. Land: Thomas CARPENTER, Thomas HOWARD. Wit: John PONDER, James WILSON (son/ William P.). Bond: William MARSHALL.

pg 133

WARREN, Eunice   Broadkiln H.   23JUN1853   17JAN1854
Grson: Lodawick W. ATKINS (has dau Aletta Catherine). Grdau: Elizabeth VENT (wife/ William S. (EX)). Mentioned: Lodawick WARREN (dec) (grfa/ L.W. ATKINS). Wit: John PONDER, Thomas W. WALLS, Thomas WALKER

pg 134

HURDLE, Jacob   Ind Riv H.   10APR1843   19JAN1854
Sons: William W.(EX), Joseph C. (EX), Jacob F. (EX). Dau: Eliza A. Wit: Peter WALLS, James WALLS.

pg 136

LINGO, Henry   Ind Riv H.   8JUN1843   19JAN1854
Wife: Eliza A. (EX-ref). Sons: Edward T., Alfred P., Andrew M., William J. (EX-ref), Samuel W. Daus: Comfort WARRINGTON, Frances Ann. Land: Daniel LINGO, Fletcher LACY, Philip MARRINER. Wit: Hammon LINGO, Jesse LINGO.

pg 138

GORDEN, David   30DEC1853   21JAN1854
Wife: Frances (EX). Bro: James. Wit: William HARRIS, Sophia LANK.

pg 139

ELLIOTT, Margaret   8MAY1853   24JAN1854
Son: Andrew W. (EX) (has wife, Mary). Grsons: George W., James T. Grdaus: Margaret E., Sarah J. Wit: Jacob WOOTTEN, Hiram W. HEARN.

pg 141

DIRECKSON, James P.   9JAN1854   1MAR1854
Wife: Mary Ann (EX). Wit: William WILLIAMS, John M. RICKARDS, Lemuel H. DIRECKSON.

pg 142

HILL, Zadoc   30NOV1852   1MAR1854
Wife: Polly (EX-ref). Rubin H. WEST ("near relation"). Wit: William S. HALL, Joseph E. HALL, Isaac COBB. Bond: Henry E. HILL, William H. LEGGETT.

7

pg 144

WALLS, William   Nanticoke H.   farmer   2SEP1851   21MAR1854
Wife: Eliza. Sons: James Mitchell (U21), Asa (dec), James D. (dec). Daus: Sally SHARP (wife/ Thomas (EX)).
Celia POTTER (widow/ Benjamin Jr). Grsons: William Burton (son/ Asa), William Zacheriah & James Henry
(sons/ James D.), William JACKSON & James JACKSON (sons/ Julius A. JACKSON. Land: Charles ARGOE,
Cedar Creek H., Charity POLK, Sarah POLK, Abraham DANIEL, Henry HUDSON. Wit: Caleb S. LAYTON,
Alfred SHORT, Caleb Rodney LAYTON.

pg 147

MARVILL, Theodore W.   Ind Riv H..   23MAR1852   28MAR1854
Wife: Catherine.. Son: Nathaniel H. Mentioned: Letty ADKINS (wife/ James). Land: Broadkiln H. Wit: D..B..
TINKER, Joshua H. EVANS, Joseph MORRIS. Bond: Manean B. MARVEL, Peter R. BURTON.

pg 149

WOLFE, Reece   15DEC1853   28MAY1854
Wife: Lydia (EX). Son: John. Dau: Lydia (U12). Appraisers: Joseph H. DODD, John N. HOOD, Thomas
WALKER. Wit: Thomas WALKER, Mary WALKER. Bond: John WOLFE, Dennis WOLFE.

pg 151

PANE, Lorenzo D.   14APR1854   1MAY1854
Wife: Mary (EX). Bro: Gove. Sis: Leah. Nephew: Thomas. Men: Elijah HITCH (son/ Henry). Wit: Samuel
LAWS, Charles H. ADAMS, Henry HITCH.

pg 152

LANK, Mitchell   Lewes & Rehoboth H.   28OCT1853   1MAY1854
Sons: John C. (EX), James (EX-ref), William J. (EX-ref). Wit: J. D. RODNEY. P. B. NORMAN.

pg 154

DALE, Eli   Worchester Co MD   8APR1852   18OCT1853   Pro Sus 8MAY1854
Sons: Josiah Tull (EX), James Simpson (EX), John Bayard. Dau: Rhoda Jane. Father: Jesse. Grson: Charles
Showell. Cousin: John M. (EX). Land: William FREENY, Elisha DAVIS. Isaac BRIDDLE (dec), Thomas G.
LAWS, Eli DAVIS, Johnson GRAY. Wit: James WHALEY, Edward N. WILLIAMS, Edward T. WHALEY.

pg 158

MURRAY, William Sr.   Worchester Co MD   WD 26JAN1854   1FEB1854   Pro Sus 8MAY1854
Wife: unnamed. "lately deceased". Sons: Laban H. (EX), Stephen W. Daus: Margaret BEVANS, Rachel
MORRIS, Amy. Men: Joseph LONG's burying place. Land: Wilson MC NEAL, James HICKMAN, Joseph MC
CABE (dec), James DAISEY. Wit: James A. HUDSON, Josiah T. SELBY, Ebe BISHOP.

pg 160

WATSON, David   Cedar Cr H.   1MAY1854   1JUL1854
Sons: David S. (EX), James T. Dau: Nelly (wife/ David S.). Grson: Henry H. HUDSON. Grdau: Martine
HICKMAN. Hsekpr: Lydia HUDSON (widow). Land: Lemuel B. SHOCKLEY, Manlove JOHNSON, Manlove B.
CARLISLE (has wife). Jonathan MILMAN. Wit: Luke ELLINGSWORTH. Manlove JOHNSON. Bond:
Lodawick WARREN.

pg 163

FOOKS, Sally wid/ Thomas Sr   Broad Cr H.   21JUN1854   19JUL1854
Son: Isaac N. Daus: Nancy HOPKINS, Eleanor HUDSON, Lavinia COTTINGHAM (wife/ Alfred). Elizabeth
WILSON (wife/ David M.), Mary Ann JAMES (wid/ Hiram H.), Gincy V. BACON (wid/ Jonathan), Sally JONES
(wife/ Thomas A.), Priscilla W. Grsons: Isaac N. F. HOPKINS (son/ Nancy), Thomas F. & Edwaard W. HUDSON
(sons/ Eleanor). Grdaus: Sally Ann & Mary Eliza HOPKINS (daus/ Nancy), Lucinda J., Mary E., & Sarah W.
JAMES (daus/ Sally JONES). Wit: W.W. MORGAN, Julia A. MESSICK. Bond: Robert S. JAMES.

pg 165

TRUITT, Caleb negro 13NOV1846 17JUL1854
Wife: Esther. Daus: Ketturah, Leah TEN. Grsons: Leven, Caleb. Grdau: Eliza Jane SHORT. Son-law: William SHORT (has son John Henry, U18). EX- Anderson TRUITT. Wit: James HOPKINS, Josiah H. MELSON.

pg 167

DAVIDSON, James Ind Riv H. 8FEB1853 21JUL1854
Wife: unnamed. Sons: Lemuel (EX), Nathan W., Samuel, James H., John W. Daus: Sarah T. THOROUGHGOOD (wife/ William N.), Charlotte, Mary T., Eliza Ann MC GEE (dec) (wife/ Levin J.) Grdau: Eliza Ann MC GEE (U?1, dau/ Eliza Ann & Levin J.) Wit: L.P. HAMMOND, Jacob B. KIMMEY.

pg 168

GREEN, John Ind Riv H. 6JUN1854 7AUG1854
Wife: Lydia. Sons: Benjamin B., William B. (EX), George W. Daus: Leah R., Arcada C., Eliza H., Hetty R. JOSEPH (wife/ William C.). Grch: Pulina, Gardner H., Maranda, Dolphus, & Amelia JOSEPH (ch/ Thomas T. JOSEPH, all U21). Grsons: Henry JOHNSON, George SIMPLER. Grdaus: Elen JOHNSON, Lucy SIMPLER, Susan Emely GREEN (all U21). Wit: James F. BURTON, Moses MEGEE. Bond: James RUST.

pg 170

WARRINGTON, Benjamin S. Ind Riv H. 9JUL1854 14AUG1854
Dau: Eliza Jane. Bros: William T. (EX), James D. (dec). Sis: Sophia S. TRUITT (wife/ David S.). Sis-law: Elizabeth (widow/ James D.). Nephews: John Wesley, James Henry & William Benjamin (all U21, sons/ James D.). Niece: Sarah Ann (U21, dau/ James D.) Mentioned: William PALMER "neighbor & friend", Hester DODD, Rev. Cornelius H. MUSTARD (pastor/ Cool Spring Church), "family burying ground". Land: Robert BURTON (dec). Benjamin ROBINSON. Wit: James F. BURTON, James F. MARTIN.

pg 172

MORRIS, Joseph 26FEB1849 25AUG1854
Wife: Tabitha. Sons: Levin (EX-ref), Michael (EX). Dau: Heeldy C. LAYTON (wife/ C. R.). Grsons: Pemberton LAYTON, John MORRIS (son/ John). Grdaus: Essebel LAYTON (dau/ Robert), Nancy LAYTON, Lucy H. MORRIS, Jane MORRIS. Land: Serous WILLIAMS. Wit: Isaac COLLINS, Sampson SELBY, Amos MC CABE.

pg 175

POOL, Perry Baltimore H. 9JUL1854 18SEP1854
Wife: Ketturah P. Sons: Henry W. (EX), Erasmus M., Alfred P., Joshua R., John W. , Robert W. Daus: Rebecca A., Ketturah J. (8 youngest ch). Father-law: Benjamin RICKARDS (dec) Men: Mary H. COLLINS, Benjamin R. POOL. Land: Uriah THOMAS, Zadock AYDELOTTE, Justus ANDREWS (negro). Wit: Stephen C. AYDELOTTE, George R. TRUITT.

pg 177

CARY, Nehemiah Cedar Cr H. 13SEP1854 19SEP1854
Sons: Cornelius J., Eli B. Daus: Mary PRETTYMAN, Susan STEPHENSON, Angelina ROACH, Clarencia TAYLOR, Sarah ENNIS (wife/ Jesse), Hester Ann HOOD (wife/ James). Appraisers: John C. HAZZAARD, James W. JONES (EX), Valentine BAKER. Wit: Valentine BAKER, John ABBOTT.

pg 179

DARTER, Sally Broad Cr. H. 3APR1850 17OCT1854
Sons: James, Samuel, Gilly, Hiram, Whitefield (EX), Randolph. Daus: Betsey TURNER, Abi PLUMMER. Grson: Hudson PLUMMER. Men: Baptist Church - Benson's Meeting House. Wit: W.W. MORGAN, Margaret WAINWRIGHT. Bond: George H. VINCENT.

pg 181

WATSON, Daniel F. Little Creek H. 10APR1854 5OCT1854
Sis: Mary HEARN (wife/ Nehemiah). Nephew: William HEARN (son/ Mary). Men: John ADAMS (has wife Catherine, lives OH). Wit: Colliins W. MARVELL, William B. RECORDS. Bond: Elisha PENUEL.

9

pg 183
PHILLIPS, Thomas   Dags. H.   22DEC1853   31OCT1854
Wife: Naomi. Sons: Thomas S., John C. (EX). Daus: Mary DUKES (wife/ Paynter), Elizabeth, Nancy T. Grsons: Thomas P. & John H. DUKES (both U22). Land: Levin HOPKINS, Joseph PHILLIPS, Benjamin MELSON, Burton PHILLIPS. Wit: Joseph PHILLIPS, Lemuel DAVIDSON. Bond: Elihu G. PHILLIPS.

pg 186
MASSEY, Alexander   17AUG1854   16NOV1854
Wife: Sarah Jane. Son: John Alexander. Daus: Sarah Catherine, Charity Jane, Rina Geneva. Father-law: John TUNNELL (EX). Wit: Thomas WALKER, John N. HOOD. Bond: William HITCH.

pg 188
HOWARD, Thomas   Lewes   11NOV1854   4DEC1854
Wife: unnamed. Sons: Robert (EX), Thomas (EX), Richard (EX-ref). Dau: Margaret. Grdau: Eliza Delaware HOWARD. Wit: J.D. RODNEY, William M.S. RICKARDS. Bond: Robert WEST.

pg 190
DAVIS, Thomas   Cedar Cr H.   13FEB1854   12DEC1854
Wife: Hester S. Sons: Robert H. (EX), Thomas J. (EX). Dau: Mary M. BURTON. Grsons: Beniah & Robert Y. WATSON (sons/ Curtis S. WATSON , both U21). Men: Elijah HUDSON (dec), tombstones/ father, mother, former wife, 4 children. Land: South Milford, Samuel BRITTINGHAM, Copes Matthew FOUNTAIN, Benjamin RILEY (dec), Henry DAVIS (negro), Elzey GROVES (dec) (negro), Clement DANIEL (negro), William WATSON Sr., Curtis S. WATSON, Joseph MORGAN, George BENNETT Sr., Puurnal TOWNSEND (dec). Wit: Henry J. PIERCE, George R. FISHER.

pg 193
KOLLOCK, George   Georgetown   24OCT1840   18DEC1854
Daus: Mira PENNEWELL, Elizabeth BUTLER (wife/ James), Mary PURNAL (wife/ James), Catherine JONES, Martha HAMMOND (wife/ William). Grson: George PENNEWELL (son/ Mira). Bro: James P.W. (EX). Land: Thomas FISHER. Wit: David R. SMITH, William JEFFERSON (now dec). Aaron MARVEL attests to signature. Bond: William S. SHORT.

pg 196
VESSELS, William F.   farmer   7AUG1852   14DEC1854
Wife: Charlotte (EX). Son: Myers B. (EX). Bro: Nathaniel W. Sisters: Elizabeth PRETTYMAN, Mary BURTON, Ann , Hetty (last 2 live OH). Trust: Benjamin BURTON, John Nyliard BURTON, David BURTON, Peter R. BURTON. Wit: Lewes WEST, Robert WEST. Bond: Samuel P. BURTON, Joshua PHILLIPS, Joseph MORRIS.

pg 198
CLIFTON, Catherine   Nanticoke H.   7NOV1854   3JAN1855
Father: Pemberton (dec). Bro: Pemberton / Kent Co. (EX). Sis: Louisa C., Elizabeth, Levina PRETTYMAN. Men: Benton PRETTYMAN. Wit: Nehemiah M. SLAYTON, Joshua GRIFFITH.

pg 199
LECATT, Winder   11OCT1854   6FEB1855
Wife: Sharlotte. "my children" - unnamed. Wit: Archelaus HASTING, Jonaathan J.B. FOOKS, William N. HASTING.

pg 200
HALL, Lemuel A. Sr.   Baltimore H.   9JUL1851   13FEB1855
Wife: Sarah (EX). Sons: John C., Lemuel A. Jr. (EX), Thomas E., Philip W., Charles. (U21), Joseph M. Dau: Sarah H. BISHOP. Grson: Lemuel A. HALL. Land: State of Missouri, Isaac C. WEST, John TAYLOR, Stephen R. EVANS, James DERECKSON, Enoch EVANS (dec). Wit: William S. HALL, David GODWINE.

pg 203

KINDER, Isaac   28OCT1848   27FEB1855
Wife: Roda. Sons: Warren (EX), John, Daniel B., Jacob. Dau: Sina WRIGHT (wife/ Lewes N.)/ Men: "family burying ground". Land: Joseph BYERS, Owens KINDER, John H. TREFORD, Solomon NOBLE, Alexander NOBLE, Solomon FRAMPTON, Elijah CANNON, Clement LAYTON. Wit: Thomas JACOBS, Henry Clay DOUGLASS. Bond: Nathaniel HORSEY.

pg 205

COLLINS, George   Broadkiln H.   18FEB1855   27FEB1855
Bro: Eli Saunder (EX). Sis: Sarah ABBOTT. Nephews: William T., John A., Eli L. (sons/ Eli). Land: David HAZZARD. Wit: Asa CONWELL, Lydia A. JOHNSON, James W. JONES.

pg 206

MAULL, Peter   Lewes   1APR1852   8MAR1855
Wife: Mary (EX). Son: Joseph (EX). Dau: Lyddy HICKMAN. Wit: Samuel E. PAYNTER, Richard PAYNTER. Bond: John METCALF.

pg 208

JOSEPH, William E.   Ind Riv H.   23FEB1855   7MAR1855
Wife: Elizabeth W. (EX-ref). Sons: Thomas Alfred (EX), Willard Wiltbank. Daus: Eliza Ann, Emely, Catherine Ellon, Maranda Short Wit: Manaen B. MARVEL, Paynter JOSEPH.

pg 209

JOHNSON, Ananias B.   Dags H.   31JAN1854   27MAR1855
Wife: Polly (EX). Sons: Robert M., Wingate, John B., Benjamin (EX). Daus: Hetty HICKMAN, Louisa ELLIOTT, Lovy S., LECATT. Grson: John WINGATE (son/ Lovy LECATT). Land: Hiram S. SHORT, Thomas W. JOHNSON, Cornelius WAPLES (dec). Wit: Greensbery ROGERS, Lemuel DAVIDSON.

pg 212

SHANKLAND, Mary   wid/ William   Lewes   JAN1855   10MAY1855
Mentioned: Eliza Mustard & Caroline Mustard BENTON (daus/ Ann M. MARSH & John H. BENTON (dec). Ann M. MARSH (wife/ Dr. Joseph MARSH. Mary A. , Clementine E.W., & Louisa H. WARNER (daus/ John PARKER.(dec). Alice BURTON (colored). George PARKER (dec). John H. PARKER. Edward L. PARKER (EX). George H. PARKER. Henry WOLFE (EX). Wit: William M.S. RICKARDS, Jesse T. POOL. Bond: William P. ORR.

pg 214

PENTON, James   Broad Cr H.   7MAY1855   22MAY1855
Wife: Elizabeth. Sons: Mathias, William D., James. Daus: Elizabeth WHITE (wife/ Purnal), Tency MOORE (wid/ William), Catherine LOYD (wife/ Joshua), Susan, Mary, Sarah PENTON (wife/ William), Zipporah HUSTON (wife/ Elisha (EX)). Wit: Wesley MORGAN, Boaz BELL.

pg 216

FURMAN, Jehu B.   Baltimore H.   7MAY1855   29MAY1855
Wife: Gatty J. Sons: George P. (U18), Edward J. Daus: Hetty Jane, Amanda, Laura Ann, Martha T., Lousenda (all U18). EX- James FURMAN. Land: John BARRON. Wit: Joshua T. LYNCH, Peleg W. HELM. Bond: Henry HICKMAN.

pg 219

MITCHELL, Elijah   7MAR1855   29MAY1855
Wife: Saly (EX). Sons: Samuel, James (EX), Rufus. Daus: Rachel (wife/ Samuel), Hetty. Grson: Rufus (son/ Samuel & Rachel). Men: Hyram J. MITCHELL (son/ Burton), Isaac S. MITCHELL, Luranah LEWIS. Land: Thomas TRUITT, James MITCHELL, Joseph PARKER. Wit: Isaac L. JEARMAN, James E. JERMAN, Thomas TRUITT.

11

pg 221

ROSS, Sarah   3SEP1850   8JUN1855
Men: Eunice ROSS (widow), Georgeanna HAZZARD. William HAZZARD (EX). Wit: Theophelus COLLINS, John STREET (now dec).

pg 222

BRITTINGHAM, John   Cedar Cr H.   12AUG1852   9JUN1855
Wife: Elizabeth (EX). Son: Samuel H. (EX-ref). Dau: Mary E. Wit: Humphries BROWN, George R. FISHER. Bond: William SHORT.

pg 224

PHILLIPS, Hosea B.   30APR1855   12JUN1855
Bros: George, Thomas. Aunt: Elizabeth RALPH. Father, mother (dec). Wit: Isaac GILES, James C. LOWE.

pg 225

WRIGHT, Frettwell   Broadkiln H.   31JAN1855   3JUL1855
Wife: Margret. Son: Peter F. Men: Dr. David HOUSTON. EX- Elisha HOLLAND. Land: Nathaniel HICKMAN, Charles KING (dec), Samuel C. PAYNTER (dec). Wit: Elisha HOLLAND, Louisa A. HOLLAND. Bond: John RODNEY.

pg 227

DAWSON, Bayard   NWF H.   19MAY1855   3JUL1855
:Surviving children" EX- Dr. William MORGAN. Wit: Purnal WHITE, Levin MOORE, Edward A. COLLINS. Bond: James SCOTT.

pg 228

BURTON, David   Millsboro   22JUN1855   10JUL1855
Dau: Virginia C. (U21). Bros: Benjamin (EX), John H. Peter R. Wit: Gardner H. WRIGHT, Job J. WINGATE.

pg 230

WILSON, Col. John   NWF H.   3OCT1849   10JUL1855
Wife: Ann. Son: William B. /Bridgeville. Dau: Mary Ann MACKLIN (wife/ John, EX). Grson: David (son/ William B.). Men: Dr. Benjamin HUDSON. Land: John Burton WINGATE, Joseph WATSON, Jes POLK (negro), George WILLIAMS (negro). Wit: Stansbury CANNON, John JONES. Bond: John D. RODNEY.

pg 232

COLLINS, Elizabeth widow   Nanticoke H.   8FEB1848   6AUG1855
Father: Dr. Adam CLARK. Sons: Joseph A. (EX), George Washington (EX), Samuel W., Francis (dec). Grdaus: Ann Eleanor, Elizabeth Agnes, Maria Emely, Martha Jane, Mary Hester aka Mary Frances (daus/ Francis, all U18). Wit: William HAZZARD, Stephen M. MORGAN. Cod: 27OCT1855: Wit: Lot RAWLINS, Philip H. RAWLINS. Cod: 29MAY1855 Grdau: Ann Eleanor now married. Wit: Lot RAWLINS, Philip H. RAWLINS, Stephen MORGAN. Cod: 31MAY1855. Wit: Lot RAWLINS, Stephen MORGAN, M.A. MORGAN.

PG 240

GORDY, John (son/ I.)   Laurel, Little Cr H.   10AUG1855   17SEP1855
Wife: Mary M. (EX). Bro: Seth. Men: George BUNTING, Frankling BUNTING (sons/ Thomas J. GORDY). Wit: J.W. SIRMAN, George HORSEY, C..C. WINDSOR. Bond: William W. DASHELL.

pg 242

CANNON, John   NWF H.   14MAY1855   9AUG1855
Wife: Hester Ann (EX-ref). Sons: Barthallomew M., Charles Franklin, George W., James M. Dau: Mary Virginia. Wit: William K. JACOBS, Ann B. CADE, Wesley SMITH. Bond: William CANNON.

12

pg 244

TILNEY, John   Broadkiln H.   13JUN1852   15AUG1855
Wife: Hannah (EX-ref). Son: Robert H. Dau: Aletta WILSON (wife/ William R..). Nephews: John, William &
Peter (sons/ Robert W. TILNEY). Land: Milton, Samuel HURT (dec). Wit: George HALL,, Nathan CLIFTON.
EX- John C. HAZZARD. Bond: William A. HAZZARD, Charles VAUGHAN.

pg 246

ELZEY, Mary (widow/ Robert) Little Cr. H.   21JUL1855   14AUG1855
Bros: Thomas & William RALPH. Men: Mary ELLIS (wife/ William), Alfred ELZEY, Mary NOBLE (wife/
James). EX- William ELLIS (son/ William). Wit: Stephen GREEN, James PUSEY, Cyrus C. WINDSOR. Bond:
George W. ELLIS, James ELLIS.

pg 248

BURTON, Robert H.   Ind Riv H.   22AUG1855   3SEP1855
Bro: Edward (EX). Wit: Sarah A. BURTON, James F. BURTON.

pg 249

SPICER , Tilghman   Broad Cr H.   7OCT1852   18SEP1855
Sons: Tilghman L. (EX), Elzey, John E., William W., Curtis. Daus: Dolly, Mahala WAINWRIGHT, Elizabeth
LOYD. Men: "family burying ground". Land: Isaac KNOWLES, Richard DURHAM (dec) / Nanticoke H.),
John DAY, John DURHAM. Wit: William HAZZARD, W..N. MORGAN.

pg 251

CAREY, Elisha   25AUG1855   4SEP1855
Son: William H. Daus: Jincy HALL, Mary, Hester Ann NICHOLSON. Grsons: Cornelius Ristine COULTER,
William , Henry & James EVANS, James & William CAREY, Nehemiah C. & James H. NICHOLSON. Grdaus:
Eliza EVANS, Hester Ann & Mary CAREY (daus/ William). EX-ref- John C. HAZZARD. Wit: John DAVIS,
James REDDEN. Bond: William W. DONOVAN.

pg 253

STOCKLEY, Hannah R.   Georgetown   10JUN1845   11SEP1855
Son: Charles C. (EX). Daus: Elizabeth TUNNELL (wife/ George), Emeline BRINKLOE (widow). Men: William
& Charles BRINKLOE (sons/ John P. BRINKLOE) (both U21). Land: Dr. John MARTIN. Wit: Martha F.
TORBERT, James P.W. KOLLOCK, Mira WRIGHT. Bond: John WEST.

pg 255

WARREN, Samuel   Nanticoke H.   23AUG1855   10DEC1855
Wife: Nancy. Sons: Kendal S., John, Robert. Daus: Hester REYNOLDS, Mary Ann, Sarah Ann (U21), Nancy
(U21). Grson: Samuel REYNOLDS. Men: "burying ground"/ Asbury Meeting House. Land: Josiah
PRETTYMAN, Peter PRETTYMAN, Paynter PRETTYMAN, Miles DICKERSON, David HAZZARD, Outen MC
CALLY (has wife), Broadkiln H. EX-ref: Elias S. RICKARDS. Wit: John WEST, Charles H. RICHARDS.
Bond: John P. GRUNDY, Thomas B. SEPPLE.

pg 259

DEPUTY, Zacheriah   21JUN1843   4JAN1856
Wife: Sarah. Son: James Henry. Bros: Joshua (dec), Sylvester. Nephews: Zacheriah (son/ Joshua), James Henry
(EX) (son/ Sylvester). Wit: Alfred LOFLAND, Isaac CARPENTER. Bond: William PORTER.

pg 260

DIRICKSON, Levin H.   10AUG1855   12JAN1856
Wife: Matilda (EX). Sons: Peter. M., Benjamin D.B., Levin H. Joseph M. Daus: Sarah B. LYNCH, Hetty C.,
Matilda A. Wit: N.W. EVANS, Joshua J. EVANS. Bond: Jehu B. DERECKSON.

WILLIAMS, Nathan   28JAN1851   15JAN1856
Wife: Hester (EX-ref).   Men: William R. WILLIAMS (has ch), Mary Holland HICKMAN, Elizabeth Ann
HICKMAN, Tabitha HICKMAN, Robert RICKARDS, Sarah DICKERSON.   Wit: James L. WILLIAMS, Elizabeth
BRASHER, Lemuel S. WILLIAMS, Benton H. BRASHER.   EX- Joshua T. LYNCH.   Bond: Robert RICKARDS.

ELLIOTT, Meshack   Laurel   29NOV1853   23FEB1856
Wife: Margarett.   Dau: Mary Ann.   Son-law: Theophilus COLLINS (EX).   Wit: Elihu I. PUSEY (moved from
DE), John GORDY (dec, son/ I.), Joseph BACON.   Bond: Warren KINDER, William HITCH.

NEAL, Arthur   NWF H.   27DEC1855   12FEB1856
Wife: Sarah Ann.   Sons: Charles W., James A., Jonathan.   Father: William (dec).   Bro: William.   EX- Charles
NOBLE.   Wit: Matthew G. DAVIS, William NEAL (son/ I.).   Bond: Lewis N. WRIGHT, Daniel B. KINDER.

DERICKSON, Mary Ann   Baltimore H.   7FEB1856   19FEB1856
Sons: James B., Jehu B., Job H., Harbinson W.T.C.   Dau: Sarah Ann.   All ch U21.   EX- Charles D. BENNETT.
Guardian: Jehu B. DERICKSON Sr.   Wit: William S. HALL, Jehu BENNETT.

RIGGIN, Robert T.   9JAN1856   19FEB1856
Wife: Ann.   Son: Thomas.   EX- Thomas H. RIGGIN.   Wit: Daniel HEARN, John ELLEGOOD.

BELL, Nicholas H.   26NOV1855   21FEB1856
Wife: unnamed.   Son: Nicholas H.   Daus: Louisa, Harriet M. (EX), Esther W. (EX), Matilda H. CANNON.   Wit:
Thomas L. MOORE, William S. BELL, Boaz BELL.

TIMMONS, Esther   Baltimore H.   13AUG1849   22FEB1856
Sons: Isaac, Stephen.   Daus: Fanny (EX-ref), Patty DAVIS, Elizabeth DAVIS (widow), Nancy BALY, Sarah
HOLLOWAY (widow), Rebecca CARY, Margaret MELVIN..   Grsons: Dennard DAVIS, Jacob HOLLOWAY.
Men: Hester H. TIMMONS (dau/ James B.), Hester TIMMONS (dau/ Lemuel).   EX- Josiah T. SELBY.   Wit:
Sampson SELBY, Thomas T. ROGERS, Josiah T. SELBY.

PIERCE, Joshua L.   Cedar Cr H.   26NOV1850   17APR1856
Wife: Orpha (EX).   Sons: John W., Joshua G.   Dau: Orpha.   Wit: George W. WHITE, John A. HAZZARD.   Bond:
William PIERCE.

DICKERSON, Sarah wid/ Peter   Cedar Cr H.   13OCT1855   16APR1856
Son: Jacob T. (EX).   Dau: Elizabeth.   Wit: Joshua TRUITT, Alexander TRUITT, John W. TRUITT.

ROBBINS, David   18MAR1827   14MAY1856
Wife: Ann.   Sons: David Jr (EX), Mires.   Daus: Elizabeth, Mary RICHARDS (dec) (has ch), Sarah Ann, Ann
CONWELL.   Wit: John P. ROBBINS, Joseph ROBBINS.

LINGO, John C.   Ind Riv H..   29APR1856   14MAY1856
Wife: Ellener D. (EX).   Dau: Comfort H. (U21).   Father: John.   Land: Robert LONG, William C. JOSEPH.   Wit:
Arthur HAZZARD, Robert C. HAZZARD, Thomas ROBINSON.   Bond: John LINGO.

SHOCKLEY, Wilson   Cedar Cr H.   27APR1856   20MAY1856
Wife: Nancy. Sons: David W., John W. Daus: Mary PARVIS (wife/ John), Ann Eliza JEFFERSON (wife/ Samuel B. (EX)), Matilda, Lydia Ann WELCH (wife/ George). Land: William V. SHOCKLEY, Elias SHOCKLEY, William SHOCKLEY, Sr.   Wit: James WILKINS, Minos LYNCH, Lemuel B. SHOCKLEY.   Bond: Peter CALHENE.

HIGMAN, John   2DEC1851   12FEB1856
Wife: Priscilla. Sons: John Wesley (EX), Robert, Richard, Daniel. Daus: Alley SMITH (widow/ William), Betsey MORRIS (wife/ Elias), Leatitia FRAMPTON. Wit: Thomas JACOBS, Jacob KINDER, Mary KINDER

WEST, Joshua C.   Baltimore H.   11MAR1854   23FEB1856
Wife: Jenet. Sons: Joshua C., Peter W. Daus: Rachel R., Sarah C., Elizabeth Ann. Bro: Ruben (EX). Wit: Peleg M. HELM, Joshua C. TOWNSEND, Ebe TOWNSEND.

ROGERS, Lambert   Lewes   14JUN18??   24JUN1856
Son: John P. Daus: Mary Jane, Lucinda All ch U21. Nieces: Catherine & Ellen PARSELS (daus/ Ellenor (dec) (wife/ George / New York City). Men: Levin HOPKINS, Peter HOLLAND (hus/ Comfort). Guardian: William M. HICKMAN (EX).   Wit: James H. RUSSEL, Charles C. HICKMAN.   Bond: William P. ORR, Nathaniel W. HICKMAN, William T. WARRINGTON.

CANNON, Rachel   12JUN1856   22JUL1856
Dau: Margaret A. Relative: John Robert RICKARDS (EX).   Wit: George M. DAVIS, Sarah E. RICKARDS. Bond: George H. VINCENT.

CALLAWAY, Elijah   Broad Cr H.   11AUG1855   27JUL1856
Son: William. Dau: Elizabeth. EX- John MOORE. Wit: E.W. MOORE, James W. HOSKINS.

WILSON, James   Somerset Co MD   8SEP1853   pro Som 18OCT1853   pro Sus 24OCT1856
Wife: Elizabeth (EX). Bros: Ralph LOWE, Levin WILSON (dec) (has ch). Sis: Nelly HITCH, Rachel WALLER, Betsey WEATHERLEY, Eleanor BOUNDS, Ann BEDSWORTH. Men: Elizabeth Ellen LOWE (dau/ George). EX- Theodore PARSONS. Land: Salisbury MD, Spring Hill MD, Robert ELLIS, George ELLIS, Major WALLER. Wit: Levin T.H. IRVING, Levin W. NICHOLSON, Margaret E PARSONS, Hetty BELL.

JONES, Jeremiah   22FEB1854   22OCT1856
Sons: Jacob R. (EX), John F. Daus: Polly Rodney, Unicy Dunham, Jincy Spicer, Elizabeth Jesy. Son-law: Nathaniel KING (EX). Land: Benjamin HEARN. Wit: John JONES, John W. PARSONS. Bond: Southy KING.

GRIFFITH, Mary   Broadkiln H.   25JUL1850   20OCT1856
Dau: Elizabeth ROACH (wife/ John (EX)). Grdau: Mary Jane .ROACH (dau/ Elizabeth & John). Wit: Salathiel BAKER, John C. HAZZARD.

pg 303

WALLS, James P.   27DEC1855   28OCT1856
Wife: Ann M. (EX). Bros: William, Samuel B., Thomas P.(next EX), Brinkley L. Sis: Nancy JOSEPH (dec),
Sarah LAWSON (dec), Alea JOHNSON, Lydia JOHNSON, Juliana JOSEPH (wife/ Noah). Men: James A.W. &
Sophie E. BARBER (ch/ Elizabeth BARBER), Elen BARBER & Elizabeth M. CARPENTER (daus/ Samuel B.
WALLS), Ann W. JOHNSON (dau/ Samuel W. JOHNSON), Silas J. SMITH (son/ Silas (has other ch)), Elizabeth
JOSEPH, Indentured servant Henry C. BURTELL.   Land: Pruitt PETTYJOHN. Peter RUST. Job LAWLIS.
Jonathan J. WILSON. Wit: James W. LYNCH, Peter E. ATKINS. Bond: James ANDERSON.

pg 307

FOOKS, Benjamin   Laurel   10AUG1853   10NOV1856
Wife: Sarah. Sons: John (dec), Dr. Kendal (dec). Ch/ present wife: sons: Benjamin Franklin (EX), Henry Penn &
Elizabeth Jane FOOKS. Grsons: Samuel & Levin HITCH, Charles B. FOOKS (son/ John), Daniel FOOKS (U21)
(son/ Kendal). Grdaus: Ann Maria FOOKS (dau/ John), Sarah & Mary Ellener FOOKS (U21) (daus/ Kendal).
Land: Risdon MOORE, Nancy MARTIN, Charles MOORE, John MOORE, Whiting SANFORD, Manaen BULL,
Caleb ROSS. Wit: John W. HOUSTON, Southy A. POLK, John T. MOORE, George W. HORSEY.

pg 310

HOUSTON, Elizabeth   Lewes   16JUL1855   10NOV1856
Sons: Robert, John W. (EX), David H. (EX). Daus: Mary Ann GRIFFITH (wife/ Dr. Robert W. GRIFFITH /
Hannibal MO), Elizabeth H. DUNNING (widow/ Henry), Margaret H. WILSON (widow/ Dr. Simon K. WILSON).
Grch: John H., William Edwin & Clara Elizabeth DUNNING (ch/ Henry & Elizabeth DUNNING).   Land:
Concord, DE. Wit: Lemuel W. WAPLES, William P. ORR, George W. WILLEY.

pg 314

CORDRY, Josiah   Little Cr H.   18SEP1850   6NOV1856
Wife: Betsey (EX-ref). Sons: Aren, William, John (EX). Daus: Grace HASTING(wife/ David), Nancy. Wit: John
MOORE, David R. WOLFE, C.C. WINDSOR.

pg 316

DONOVAN, Wingate   Broadkiln H.   11MAR1856   27DEC1856
Wife: Nancy. Son: James Henry (U21) (EX). .Daus: Mary Ann EDINGTON, Sarah Priscilla. EX-ref- Heaveloe
NENIS. Wit: Philip WORKMAN, W.W. WOLFE. Bond: Eli DONOVAN

pg 317

COULTER, Cornelius   Milton   24SEP1855   8DEC1856
Wife: Sarah Ann. Bro: John M. (dec). Sis-law: Mary (widow/ John M.). Mother: unnamed (dec). Sis: Eliza, Hetty
WARRINGTON, Lydia BICKAM, Mary SMITH (widow/ Rev. James). Nieces: Eliza A. FISHER (widow/ John
N.), Mary Jane CONNAWAY (dau/ John M. COULTER). Men: Joshua, Sarah & Hetty COULTER (ch/ Joseph
COULTER (dec),   Jane D. ANDERSON, Mary A., Lydia J., & William R. STEPHENSON (ch/ John
STEPHENSON (dec), Cornelius C. DAVIDSON, Cornelius C. HART, Cornelius H. MUSTARD (has 4 sis).
William HAZZARD (has 3 sis) (son/ David HAZZARD(dec) / Angola), Eliza MOORE (wife/ Gaylord) (has 4 sis),
Joseph CONWELL, William A. CONWELL, Jane ROBBINS (wife/ James), Lydia SIMPLER (dau/ Lydia &
wife/ Andrew M.), Sally C. SIMPLER (dau/ Lydia & Andrew M.), Thomas COULTER (son/ William V.),
Cornelius R. COULTER, John COULTER (son/ John M.), Margaret CAREY (wife/ Joseph H. CAREY, Mary
RUSSEL (widow/ Samuel RUSSEL), William MARTIN (son/ Josiah MARTIN (dec), Nathaniel T. VEASEY.
Betsey M. HOLLAND (wife/ Andrew J.), Hetty GOSLEE (wife/ Samuel), Sally C. BLOCKSOM (dau/ Richard
BLOCKSOM), Jacob N. COFFIN, Robert COFFIN, Sally FISHER (wife/ William). Land: Methodist Burying
Ground; Milford; Robert MC FERRAN (dec); Robert M. HALL; Andrew P. HOLLAND; Gideon B. WAPLES;
Purnal SCOTT; Goshen Methodist Meeting House / Milton; Milton School Dist. #12; Cold Spring Presby.
Church; Charles MASON; R.S. BURDICK; Nehemiah D. WELCH. Trustees/ wife: John PONDER, Thomas
DAVIS. EX-ref: John PONDER. EX-William V. COULTER. Wit: James PONDER, Noble ELLINGSWORTH.
Bond: Peter CALHERN.

16

ADAMS, Eliza   Concord   18AUG1856   15JAN1857
Nephews: Dr. William W. STUART (has idiot dau), James STUART (has ch). Niece: Sidney T. CALHOUN (wife/ David (EX)). Men: George & Alexander CALHOUN (sons/ Sidney), Mary Ann OUTTEN (wife/ Daniel W.). Madalene T. & Missouri W. CALHOUN (daus/ Sidney), John M. WINDOM. Land: Michael STUART (dec), William H. WHEATLEY, Nicholas W. ADAMS, Nanticoke H. EX-ref: George H. PHILLIPS. Wit: Nutter CANNON, Mires T. CONNAWAY, Robert G. ELLEGOOD. Bond: Thomas CALHOUN, William CALHOUN

WAINWRIGHT, Philip   Broad Cr H.   29DEC1856   16FEB1857
Sons: John W., & Jacob R. both U21. Men: Charles CONNALLY / Somerset Co MD, William R. BRADLEY. EX-James W. BOYCE. Wit: S.D. VAUGHAN, Cyrus WARD, William E. HOPKINS. Bond: Josiah H. MELSON.

HOW, Rev. James C.   St George H, New Castle Co.   pastor./ St George Presby. Church
    Will 26MAY1855   pro NC Co. 28AUG1855   pro Sus 24MAR1857
Wife: Latitia. Son: John Blanchard. Bro-law: Rev. Hugh HAMILL/ Lawrenceville, NJ (EX). Land: Sussex Co DE. Anthony M. HIGGINS/ DE (EX). Barney REYBOLD/ DE (EX). Wit: William A. TATUM, John W. OSBORN.

HICKMAN, William T.   Dags H.   18MAR1857   8APR1857
Wife: Louisa (EX). Mother: Sarah F. Land: Jonathan CAREY, Manaen GUM. Wit: John DUKES, Edward C.D. KIRKPATRICK.

ELLIOTT, Joseph   farmer   Nanticoke H.   8JUN1854   13APR1857
Wife: Adaline. Sons: John, Wingate Burton. Daus: Betsey CONNAWAY (wife/ Noble (EX)), Seny ISAACS (wife/ Minos), Tabitha FLEETWOOD (wife/ William). Grsons: John Wingate & James Noble CONNAWAY (sons/ Noble). Land: John TINDAL, Joshua J. SAMPDEN. Wit: Charles M. CULLEN, William ELLEGOOD, Thomas B. SEPPLE. Bond: Nathaniel CONNAWAY.

SMITH, Joseph   Laurel   25NOV1854   13APR1857
Wife: Lydia (EX-ref). Sons: George Elmer Horsey, Joseph Franklin Pierce, Samuel Thomson (all U16). Dau: Elizabeth Joseph Earl. EX-ref: John T. MOORE. Land: Littleton FURNIS, Nicholas V. SHORT (dec). Wit: D.R. WOLFE, Jonathan. A. HEARN. EX: ????? L. HEARN. Bond: John S. BACON.

BURTON, Polly   Angola, Ind Riv H.   NWD   13APR1857
Hus: James (dec). Men: Henry H. BURTON, Sarah P. (wife/ John Hampleton BURTON (EX)). Wit: Manean B. MARVEL, John B. HAZZARD. Bond: Zadoc MILBY, Wesley W. STEPHENSON.

HOLLAND, Peter   Lewes & Rehoboth H.   30MAR1857   21APR1857
Wife: Comfort B. (EX). Wit: Robert A. LYNCH, Richard P. PAYNTER. Bond: William A. DODD.

MC CABE, Garretson   Baltimore H.   22JAN1857   27APR1857
Wife: Elizabeth. Father: unnamed (dec). Sons: John, Amos, William (EX). Daus: Elizabeth HUDSON (wife/ Nathaniel), Patience LONG (wife/ Zeno), Susan MURRY (wife/ Joshua), Charlotte COLLINS (wife/ Elisha). Land: Isaac MC CABE. Wit: Elisha M. MC CABE, Elijah MC CABE.

MARVIL, Elizabeth M.   Dags. H.   18MAR1857   15MAY1857
Sons: Philip Rodney, George Edward. Bro: William MESSICK (EX-ref). Sis: Sarah T. MESSICK. Wit: Aaron B. MARVELL, Jane S. CARPENTER. EX- Minos MESSICK. Bond: John WEST.

17

pg 347

TRUITT, John   22DEC1851   26MAY1857
Wife: Sarah. Sons: Benton P. (EX), Greensberry M. (EX). Daus: Lavinia E., Elizabeth PHILLIPS (wife/ Elihu), Louisa W. GORDY (wife/ Aren N.). Land: Isaac BURTON, Solomon SHORT, John PHILLIPS. Wit: John C. WEST, Mahala B. WEST (now dec). Bond: John C. WEST, Elihu G. PHILLIPS.

pg 349

KNOWLES, David M.   Little Cr H.   20MAR1857   16JUN1857
Wife: Amelia Ardella Emeline. Son: William Christopher Columbus (U21). Daus: Sarepta Emeline, Hester Elizabeth Augusta, ????? Rebecca. EX- William W. DASHELL (Trustee). Wit: William S. PHILLIPS, William B. RECORDS. Bond: John T. MOORE.

pg 351

WHITE, George P.   Bridgeville   28NOV1851   9JUN1857
Wife: Sophia E. (EX). Mother: unnamed. Men: George W. COLLINS, James PRETTYMAN (head clerk). Land: Jonathan OWENS. (EX-ref): Roads HAZZARD. Wit: John B. WINGATE, James PRETTYMAN Sr. Bond: William CANNON, William ELLEGOOD.

pg 353

SHARP, Mary   widow/ Jacob   28DEC1846   4JUL1857
Sons: Asa, John, Kenzey (all EX). Dau: Pinkey PETTYJOHN. Grdaus: Mary Ann PETTYJOHN, Mary Elizabeth SHARP. Men: Catherine DICKERSON (has child, Mary Ann SMITH, allegedly by Asa SHARP). Wit: William TATMAN, James STEEL (both now dec), Penelope K. STEEL. Bond: Charles H. RICHARDS.

pg 356

WATSON, Sophia   Milton   29JUN1857   7JUL1857
Men: Margaret Emma HUDSON (dau/ Henry C. & Mary Ann HUDSON), Nancy BRITTINGHAM (wife/ Elijah / Meadville, Crawford Co, PA). Land: Capt. Elias COVERDALE. EX: Charles VAUGHAN. Wit: Charles MASON, James PONDER. Bond: James COOPER.

pg 357

MOORE, David   Baltimore H.   24OCT1855   28JUL1857
Wife: Sarah. Sons: Edward D., Thomas R. (EX). Dau: Mary Ann TAYLOR. Land: Isaiah LONG, William BRASHER (dec), Robinson MOORE. Wit: Joseph B. SUDLER, Joseph S. BARNARD (now/ MO).

pg 359

CAREY, Peter   4MAR1857   28JUL1857
Wife: unnamed. Son: John H. (EX). Dau: Nancy. "other ch". Grson: Stephen Sylvester CAREY. Wit: Walter E. JEFFERSON, Jeremiah B, HUDSON.

pg 360

LONG, Joseph   Baltimore H.   16FEB1846   4AUG1857
Wife: Mahala. Sons: Joshua P., John T. (EX), Benjamin, Nathaniel. Father: unnamed (dec). Bro: John J. Daus: Delila, Ruth, Hester, Rhoda W., Bethshana, Eliza W., Ann Marien, Mary Jane. Wit: Zeno P. LONG, William CAMPBELL, William S. MC CABE.

pg 363

RALPH, Thomas Sr.   20NOV1830   4AUG1857
Mother: Mary (dec). Bros: William Sr. (EX), Charles. Nephew: Thomas (son/ Charles). Wit: George PHILLIPS, Joshua PHILLIPS (now dec), Perry B. MOORE (gone West).

pg 364

HEAVELOE, Sarah   Broadkiln H.   3AUG1857   17AUG1857
Grson: Cornelius LOFLAND. Grdaus: Margaret ABBOTT, Matilda WARREN. Wit: Philip WORKMAN, Robert B. WORKMAN. Bond: Robert H. WARREN.

18

pg 365
HENRY, Sarah 8AUG1849 18AUG1857
Sons: William M. / OH, John (EX). Grch: Stephen P. & Martha E. HENRY. Wit: William WALLER, William
A.R. PHILIPS, George PHILIPS.

pg 368
DICKERSON, James B. 9JUL1857 18AUG1857
Wife: Nancy (EX). Son: Samuel James. Dau: Mary Ann. Niece: Frances MC ILVAIN (raised by them). Wit:
James F. MARTIN, Peter HOPKINS. Bond: Nehemiah D. WELCH.

pg 369
KINNEY, Joshua Little Cr H. 15JUL1857 19AUG1857
Wife: Sarah. Sons: James Edward, Waitman W., Samuel. Daus: Salley, Amey, Mary. EX- William B.
RECORDS. Wit: James COLLINS, Noah PHILLIPS. Bond: James T. MOORE.

pg 371
DRAIN, Sheperd 24JUN1856 27AUG1857
Wife: Sally. Sons: Albert, Lorenzo D., Stanford, Shepherd. Daus: Margaret FRISH, Susanna EKRIDGE. EX-
George W. DRAIN. Wit: Jonathan MOORE, Augustus THOMPSON, William RIGGIN.

pg 373
CLIFTON, Levica Cedar Cr H. 27JUN1857 3SEP1857
Sis: Elizabeth Pherson(?) CLIFTON, Sally Cary STEPHENS. EX- James HOUSTON. Wit: James W. CLIFTON,
Pemberton CLIFTON, Asa S. CLIFTON. Bond: John W. CLIFTON.

pg 374
MEGEE, Thomas Ind Riv H. 6JUN1857 2SEP1857
Wife: Elon. Sons: Levin J., John W., Thomas P., Noah W. (EX), William F., Peter. Daus: Mary, Elizabeth
SIMPLER. Grsons: David Cornelius MEGEE (son/ Mary), Thomas James MEGEE (son/ John W.), Charles R. &
George S. SIMPLER, William Thomas MEGEE (son/ Peter), Charles MEGEE (son/ Noah). Men: Jane MEGEE
(wife/ John W.), Patience MEGEE (wife/ Noah W.), Rhoda MEGEE (wife/ William F.). Land: Joseph ENNIS,
John BURBAYGE (dec), John MEGEE (dec), William JEFFERSON, Joseph C. HURDLE, Thomas RUST,
William W. JOHNSON, William ATKINS, Patience WALLS.. Wit: John S. SALMONS, Lemuel DAVIDSON.

pg 379
ATKINS,, James Ind Riv H. 18FEB1855 22SEP1857
Wife: Hetty (aka Aletta) EX-ref. Wit: Benjamin BURTON, George FOOKS. EX- Thomas ROBINSON (son/ A.).

pg 380
JACOBS. Stansbury NWF H. 20AUG1857 22SEP1857
Wife: Henrietta EX-ref. Sons: John W., Curtis M. (EX-ref), Rufus R., Romelus, Luther F., William K. Dau: Sally
WELLS (wife/ Edward). Grson: Stansbury JACOBS (son/William K.) Wit: Wesley SMITH, Clement CANNON,
Nancy CADE, Laurenson SMITH. EX- Wesley SMITH. Bond: William H. ROSS.

pg 383
OWENS, Thomas Broad Cr H. 26DEC1853 24SEP1857
Wife: Jane. Sons: Elijah (EX), James H. Daus: Matilda RIGGIN, Maria BAKER. Wit: John ELLEGOOD, John
MOORE, E.W. MOORE.

pg 384
WALLS, Nehemiah Ind Riv H. 19FEB1856 5OCT1857
Wife: Margaret. Sons: Renattus Thomas, David, Nehemiah W. "daughters" Grson: Nehemiah O. BAYNUM.
Grdau: Mary Jane WALLS (wife/ Gideon). Sons-law: Henry O. BENNUM (EX-ref), John WALLS (EX). Wit:
N.P. HARRIS, Joseph T. ADAMS. Bond: Henry O. BENNUM.

pg 386

SWAIN, John   Nanticoke H.   27MAR1856   7NOV1857
Wife: Polly. Sons: Walter, John Hudson (EX). Daus: Maria STEEL (eld), Betsey SMITH, Priscilla. Mary Ann.
Men: Joshua MC COLLY, William Ross MC COLLY, Betsy Evans MC COLLY (mor/ William Ross). Wit: James
D. PRETTYMAN, Thomas B. SEPPLE.

pg 388

RICHARDSON, Letitia   Nanticoke H.   4APR1854   10NOV1857
Son: William Henry. Dau: Sally SPANISH. Grdaus: Ann Matilda & Mary Elen NUTTER (both U21), Seshey
Ann SPANISH. Land: Waitman WILLEY, William WILLEY. Wit: Joshua SHARP, Charles RICKARDS.

pg 390

MOORE, James   Dags H.   5AUG1857   1DEC1857
Wife: Nancy. Son: John W. Daus: Cathern BRASHER, Jenetta SAMPSON, Mary HAZZARD, Charlotte LEWIS.
Letty A. SHORT. Son-law: Joseph LEWIS (EX). Wit: John W. RADISH, James E. BLIZZARD.

pg 391

KNOWLES, William   Little Cr H.   11APR1857   14DEC1857
Wife: Arcada. Sons: William W., Ephraim (dec, has ch). Daus: Mary A., Patience WRIGHT (has ch), Hetty E.
MORINE. Bro: Wilson (EX). "last marriage". Wit: C.C. WINDSOR, W.W. DASHIELL. Bond: Henry BACON.

pg 395

WINGATE , Hezekiah.   NWF H.   7MAR1856   17DEC1857
Wife: Nancy. Sons: Stansbery J., Elijah, John B., Isaac Newton C. Daus: Sally DAWSON (widow/ Joseph),
Tabitha KNOWLES (wife/ John), Hester L. NICHOLS (wife/ James), Nancy D. JONES (wife/ Clement). Grdau:
Nancy ELLENSWORTH (wife/ David). EX- Uanum KINDER. Land: John GOSLIN, Thomas JACOBS, Sarah C.
JACOBS, Bell Jane SMITH (wife/ Laurenson), John KINDER, Warren KINDER, Isaac BRADLEY (dec), Daniel
CANNON. Wit: Cornelius F. CANNON, Tilghman D. KINDER. Bond: John KINDER.

pg 398

HAZZARD, Arthur   Ind Riv H.   19OCT1857   4JAN1858
Father & Mother buried/ St. George's Chapel. Bros: Thomas, John B.. (EX), Richard, Robert. Sis: Ann   C.
Nephew: William Arthur HAZZARD (son/ Thomas). Cousin: David HAZZARD (son/ Joseph/ Phila). Men: John
H. BURTON (son/ James). Land: Dagworthy DERICKSON. EX-ref: John LINGO. Wit: George ROBINSON,
Thomas ROBINSON.

pg 400

PENUEL. Jane   Little Cr H.   3MAR1856   6JAN1858
Son: Josiah W. (EX). "my ch" Wit: Alexander C. MOREAU, W.B. RECORDS.

PG 402

WHARTON, John W.   Georgetown   14JUL1857   12JAN1858
Wife: Martha D. Sis: Hetty Ann FOOKS (wife/ Thomas A.). Land: Dagsborough H.. Isaac A. HOUSTON, Burton
J. WINGATE. Laban L. LYONS. EX- Robert B. HOUSTON/ Dags H. Wit: John R. MC FEE. Charles C.
STOCKLY.

pg 404

REYNOLDS, Coventon   12JUN1857   21JAN1858
Wife: Mary. Sons: William, Roderick, David, Zacheriah (EX), George L. Dau: Elizabeth SHORT (wife/ Daniel).
Land: Nanticoke H. Wit: John DAVIS, Thomas B. SEPPLE. Bond: Philip C. JONES. George HARRIS.

pg 406

BENSON. William   Broadkiln H   15SEP1857   8FEB1858
Sons: John Henry (EX), James A. Parker, David. Daus: Milly Ann COLUSTER (wife/ Peter). Margaret Elizabeth.
Wit: David LOFLAND, Robert C. WHITE, Samuel M. LOFLAND. Bond: John MACKLIN.

20

pg 408

HALL, Sarah   11FEB1858   26FEB1858
Sons: Philip W., Thomas E., Charles H. Men: George & Milly HALL (colored). EX- Kendal RICHARDS. Wit: Lemuel LYNCH, David GODWINE.

pg 409

LINGO, Elenor D.   Broadkiln H.   11NOV1857   27MAR1858
Mother: Mariah RUST (has ch: William T. & Mariah E. RUST). Men: Samuel CRAIG, William CRAIG, Mary A. MARSH. EX- Absolum RUST. Wit: John C. LANK, Hannah N. LANK.

pg 411

HILL, Elizabeth   2JUN1856   29MAR1858
Daus: Sarah H. BLIZZARD, Elizabeth STEEL, Comfort B. SMULLEN, Lydia, Ann H. C???????. Grson: Samuel G. BLIZZARD (son/ Sarah), James BLIZZARD (EX). Grdau: Cordelia Elizabeth JOSEPH. Wit: Henry O. BENNUM, Harriet W. BENNUM.

pg 413

EDINGTON, William   Broadkiln H.   2FEB1858   9APR1858
Wife: Sarah. Son: John B. (EX). Daus: Mary Jane, Sarah Ann (U18), Elizabeth MACKLIN. Wit: Thomas WALKER, Nehemiah D. WELCH. Bond: Ebenezer P. WARRINGTON.

pg 415

MOORE, Mary   6OCT1857   14APR1858
Father: unnamed, estate of. Daus: Julia Ann, Hester Annet, Mary E. MARVEL. Men: Collins W. MARVEL, Amelia Patience MARVEL (dau/ Collins). EX- Jesse A.D. BRADLEY. Wit: B.W. ROADS, C.C. BRADLEY.

PG 417

WALLACE, Rev. James L.   8DEC1856   11MAY1858
Wife: Phaney H. (EX). Adopted Son: James L. WALLACE (son/ Samuel & Eleanor OLIVER/ Laurel, both dec). Adopted Dau: Mary H. FISHER (dau/ John , dec, & Eliza Ann FISHER/ Milton). Father: James L. (dec). Sis: Eliza KNOWLES, Margaret DOWNING, Rebecca IINSLEY. Land: Jonathan HEARN/ Laurel (has wife), Joseph MOORE (has wife). Wit: John T. MOORE, John M.C. HEARN, Mary P. FOOKS. Bond: Kendal M. LEWIS.

pg 420

HOLT, William   Broad Cr H.   6APR1858   13MAY1858
Wife: Mary. Son: Miles S. (EX). Wit: Wesley MORGAN, Lemuel HASTING.

pg 421

HAZZARD, John T.   17MAR1857   21APR1858
Wife: Mary (EX). Daus: Eliza, Esther. Wit: John D. RODNEY, Mary O. RODNEY, Eliza S. RODNEY.

pg 423

WEST, John C.   14DEC1857   27MAY1858
Wife: Mary Ann (EX). Sons: William Joseph (eld), James Anderson, Samuel Burton & John Henry (youngest). Daus: Priscilla Margaret Ann (eld), Lavinia Elizabeth (U21). Land: Hezekiah MATTHEWS, Little Creek H. EX- Daniel B. CANNON. Wit: Hezekiah MATTHEWS Sr, Hezekiah MATTHEWS Jr.

pg 426

HUDSON, Benjamin son/ David   Baltimore H.   17MAR1857   3JUN1858
Wife: Polly (dec). Sons: David, Aaron H. Daus: Mary D., Elizabeth, Hetty Jane. EX- Capt. Henry HICKMAN (Trustee). Land: Samuel D. BENNETT, Jehu B. DERICKSON, Elijah LYNCH. Matilda M. DERICKSON, Nathaniel M. DERICKSON. Wit: William ELLEGOOD, A.C. PEPPER, Charles M. CULLEN. Bond: John B. WAPLES, Laban L. LYONS.

21

HEMMONS, William   20APR1858   15JUN1858
Wife: Peggy. Son: John B. (EX). Grsons: William J., Joshua M., James T., David. Wit: Charlton SMITH, John H. SATTERFIELD. Bond: William G. CARLISLE.

CRAIG, Robert   Ind Riv H.   9SEP1857   15JUN1858
Son: James D. (EX). Daus: Lydia MESSICK (wife/ Elias), Comfort C. BRYAN (wife/ Jacob). "brothers & sisters" Land: Joseph HURDLE, Samuel DAVIDSON, Robert LAWSON, Burton PRETTYMAN, Gardiner H. WRIGHT, J.S. SALMON. Wit: John PONDER, James PONDER. Bond: Burton C. PRETTYMAN.

HUFFINGTON, Rachel   Seaford   13MAR1853   8JUL1858
Men: Mary R. HILL (EX) (wife/ William T.) , William Huffington ELENSWORTH (son/ George), J.N. MOORE (constable), Mary Susan MARVEL (dau/ William & Catherine MARVEL).   Land: George HELLEN, Jacob WRIGHT, William C. ELENSWORTH. Wit: Philip O'NEAL, Eleanor BOYCE, William GILES.

WATSON, Elizabeth   Cedar Cr H.   31DEC1857   20JUL1858
Son: Curtis S. (EX) (has ch). Men: Mary E. TRUITT (dau/ John S. WATSON), Mary E. WATSON (dau/ Bethuel), Bethuel WATSON (son/ C.), Elizabeth CARLISLE (wife/ Thomas), Catherine TRUITT (wife/ John S., have ch). Wit: George W. WHITE, William PORTER

SHIRMAN, Polly   Broadkiln H.   13MAY1848   27JUL1858
Son: John (EX). Daus: Tabitha WILSON (wife/ Backley), Sary JOHNSON (wife/ Minos). Grdau: Mary Hester SHIRMAN. Wit: Peter R. JACKSON, Nancy PALMER.

O'NEAL, Pomp   Broad Cr H.   2MAY1858   28JUL1858
Wife: Pheby. "all the ch" Grson James O'NEAL. Grdau: Margaret O'NEAL. Wit: George H. VINCENT, Thomas CALHERN.

PARKER, Elizabeth   Broadkiln H.   20MAR1853   9SEP1858
Sons: James STEEL, John STEEL (EX). Dau: Elisa FISHER. Wit: David ROBINS, Elizabeth ROBINS. Bond: Philip C. JONES.

RUSSEL, William   Georgetown   30APR1853   28JUL1858
Sons: Joseph, John, William P. (EX). Daus: Mary K. SHARP, Margaret Ann MACKLIN, Matilda M. POWELL. Grsons: Isaac & Gideon W. BURTON (sons/ John & Jane K.(dec) BURTON). Grdaus: Eliza CARPENTER, Margaret Ann VAUGHAN, Frances Matilda BURTON & Sarah Ann VAUGHAN (all daus/ John & Jane BURTON). Son-law Nathaniel C. POWELL (EX). Indentured servant: John B. WAPLES negro. Land: Nanticoke H., Samuel WARREN, John RUSSEL, David HAZZARD, Theophilus COLLINS, Nutter RATCLIFF, Charles RAWLINS, John DAY, Levin COVERDALE, John P. GUNBY, John BENNETT, William W.H. HUDSON. Wit: James A. WOLFE, David W. MAULL, Abraham H. MARVEL. Bond: William H. POWELL, William SHAW.

WILLEY, Theodore   Nanticoke H.   19AUG1858   7SEP1858
Wife: Mary Ann. Sons: Simeon, Nehemiah. Dau: Mary Annie. Bro: John (EX). Wit: George M. DAVIS, Joshua WILLEY.

pg 447
DONOVAN, James R.   Broadkiln H.   23NOV1854   21SEP1858
Wife: Nancy (EX). Sons: William Theodore (EX), James R. Dau: Eliza. Men: James W. OLIVER. Land: Aaron MARSHALL, George CALHERN, James REED, Henry SHARP. Wit: William W. WOLFE, William E. WOLFE. Bond: Purnal J. PETTYJOHN.

pg 449
DEPUTY, Rachel   Milton   13MAY1858   13OCT1858
Men: Eliza Ann VAUGHAN (wife/ Edward M. (EX)), Jincy HALL (wife/ Robert M.), Hetty NICHOLS (widow/ Thomas). Wit: C.W. BURTON, John C. HAZZARD.

pg 451
WOOTTEN, Isaac   24MAY1851   18NOV1858
Son: Nathaniel J. (EX). Dau: Mary Ann DENNIS (dec) (wife/ Benjamin, they have 2 ch U21). Men: Eliza M??????? (wife/ Southy T. M???????), Phebe HEARN (wife/ Benjamin), Eleanor WILLIAMS (wife/ Luther), Sally GERMAN (wife/ John). Wit: John Turpin MOORE, George W. HENRY. Bond: Elias TAYLOR.

pg 453
WILSON, Charity   Milton   28JUL1858   10DEC1858
Bro: Julius A. JACKSON. Sis: Pinkston JACKSON. Nieces: Louisa MOORE (wife/ Thomas A. (EX)); Mary HOOPER, Elizabeth C. MALONY, & Almira MORGAN (daus/ Pinkston & Julius JACKSON). Men: Ann BAYNUM (wife/ James), Mary Emma MOORE (dau/ Louisa & Thomas A.). Wit: Joseph J. BETTS, Emeline BETTS. Bond: John T. MOORE.

pg 454
BURTON., Arcada   Ind Riv H.   22NOV1858   14DEC1858
Sons: Edward (EX), William C. (EX), Lemuel P. Land: Angola, James P.W. MARCH. Wit: James F. BURTON, Lydia BURTON. Bond: Dagworthy DERICKSON.

pg 456
HICKMAN, William   Son/ John   Cedar Cr H.   4OCT1858   29DEC1858
Wife: Sarah Ann. Sons: Caleb Joshua, William John. Daus: Mary Ann, Rachel Ann. EX-John C. HAZZARD/ Milton. Wit: William LANE, William W. WOLFE. Bond: J.C. BAYNUM.

pg 457
WILSON, Jonathan J.   Ind Riv H.   11OCT1858   4JAN1859
Wife: Ann. Sons: George F. (EX), Nathaniel H., Elias B., Kendal D., William. Father: William (dec). Grfa: Jonathan JOSEPH. Land: Benjamin MC ILVAIN, Brinkley JOHNSON, Samuel JOSEPH, Zacheriah JOSEPH, Stephen E. BLIZZARD (dec). Wit: Lizzie F. ANDERSON, Elon W. STOCKLEY, James ANDERSON.

pg 460
RUSSEL, William   Pilot Town, Lewes & Reh. H.   1AUG1857   21JAN1859
Wife: Betsey (EX). Sons: Robert R., James H., William T., Edward. Daus: Elizabeth M. RHODES, Mary P., Essie H. Land: William ARNOLD (dec), George B. RODNEY. Lewes WEST, William SCHELLENGER, Jacob R. ROWLAND, Laban L. LYONS, John METCALF, Samuel J. LODGE, Benjamin KOLLOCK, S.P. HOUSTON, Robert HOUSTON (dec), Lewes, R.R. RUSSEL, D. Rodney KING, James WEST, Thomas CARPENTER, John MARSHALL (has wife), James COLEMAN, Jacob S, BURTON, Thomas MAULL. Wit: James DUFFEL, Thomas R. DUFFEL.

pg 463
HOUSTON, John R.   14JAN1859   1FEB1859
Wife: Zilby. Sons: Elisha C. (eld) (EX), William B. (EX), Martin M., John Jr., Thomas, James. Daus: Mary COLLINS, Sarah A. COLBORN, Margaret BLOCKSOM, Milley LOYD, Eliza, July A. Land: Broad Creek H. Wit: William C. PENTON, David H. TUBBS. Bond: Joseph C. ALLEN.

pg 464

CALLAWAY, Ebenezer   21JUN1855   7FEB1859
Nephews: Elihu CALLAWAY, John CALLAWAY (son/ Isaac), William CALLAWAY. Land: Nathaniel
HORSEY , Thomas W. RECORDS, Samuel KINNEY, James E. ELLIS. EX- John L. BACON. Wit: Henry
BACON, Hardy CULVER.

pg 466

JAMES, Robert L.   Broad Cr H.   3OCT1857   18FEB1859
Wife: Mary E. (EX). Sons: Coldwell W., Rubin, Noah, Joshua. Ch: Hiram H., Catherine Wise, & Nancy Eleanor
(ch/ Mary E.). EX- Minos T. CONNAWAY. Land: George CANNON, Joshua JAMES (dec). Wit: Curtis A.
CONNAWAY, Thomas A. MEARS.

pg 468

SHORT, Gilley G.   Nanticoke H.   12JUN1856   19FEB1859
Sons: Alfred, William, Daniel B., John C. (EX), Gilly M. (EX). Daus: Elizabeth P. SMITH (wife/ Nicholas O.),
Mary Ann SWAIN (dec), Hester Ann DAY, Sinia MC COLLY. Grch: Truston, Cornelius, Leah Jane, Catherine
& Sinia SWAIN (ch/ Mary Ann). Land: Isaac N. FOOKS. Wit: Joseph A. COLLINS, Stephen M. MORGAN.
Bond: William ELLEGOOD, George HARRIS.

pg 470

BENSON, Henry   16MAY1855   1MAR1859
Wife: Betsey (EX). Sons: Charles Henry, George Hamilton. Daus: Jerusha ROACH, Eliza Ann, Sally, Caroline,
Elizabeth. Wit: Isaac OBIER, Jacob P. OBIER. Bond: Henry ROACH.

pg 472

EVANS, Isaac Sr.   Baltimore H.   1JAN1859   23MAR1859
Wife: Hetty. Sons: John M., Joshua J., Isaac, Edward D. (EX), Curtis J. (youngest). Daus: Jane T. DERICKSON.
Elizabeth DAVIS, Ann T. RICKARDS, Hester DAZEY, Catherine. "Family Bible" Land: John M. RICKARDS,
James LAWSON, Capt. William WHARTON, James M. KNOX, Capt. William HOLLAND. (EX)-Joseph E.
HALL. Wit: Lemuel W. RICKARDS, Philip H. RICKARDS, W.E. JEFFERSON. Bond: William S. HALL.

pg 474

FISHER, Dr. James H.   4MAR1859   5APR1859
Wife: Catherine G. (EX). Son: Frank. Dau: Mary Jr. Bros: Daniel G., Luther W. Land: Concord, Lewis
SPICER. Wit: James W. MORGAN, Cornelius C. JAMES. Bond: William H. WHEATLY, Thomas A. JONES.

pg 475

TAYLOR, Elizabeth   23MAR1859   12APR1859
Men: Philip James (U21) & Margaret A. SATCHEL (ch/ James). Mary E. CALLAWAY (wife/ Harry). EX- John
TAYLOR. Wit: Henry W. ELLIOTT, Thomas CALHERN. Bond: Elias TAYLOR.

pg 477

SHORT, Daniel   Nanticoke H.   21APR1854   8JUN1859
Wife: Ann. Sons: John M. (EX), Samuel T. (EX), Gilly C., Purnal W. Daus: Ann J., Elizabeth WILLEY (wife/
Edward). Grdaus: Ann E., Marie E., Elizabeth A., Mary H., & Martha J. COLLINS (all U18). Wit: Lot
RAWLINS, P.W. RAWLINS.

pg 479

DAVIS, Nehemiah   farmer   Cedar Cr H.   13JUN1850   10MAY1859
Sons: Henry (EX), Nehemiah (EX), & Thomas (by former wife). Sons: John S., Lot W. Daus: Elizabeth DAVIS
(wife/ Mark), Sarah DAVIS (dec) (by former wife). Daus: Sarah E. DRAPER (wife/ Myres), Jane TODD (dec)
(wife/ Charles), Rachel DRAPER (dec) (wife/ Radcliff). Grch: Charles, William J., Clayton H., & Hetty TODD
(ch/ Jane & Charles TODD). Grdau: Rachel Ann DRAPER (dau/ Rachel & Radcliff). Grandfa: Nehemiah
DAVIS. Wit: Daniel CURRY, Mark A. GRIER, Aaron W. BELL.

24

pg 483

TOWNSEND, Zadoc   17JUL1857   19MAY1859
Wife: Hannah. Son: James (EX). Dau: Kitty W. Grson: Zadock TOWNSEND. Wit: James M. TUNNELL, James TURNER, Elizabeth H. TURNER. Bond: Ebe WALTER.

pg 485

RUSSEL, Robert   Broadkiln H.   1856   21APR1859
Wife: Sally (dec). Wife: Mary. Sons: Alfred (EX-Trustee/ Samuel), David, William, George, Samuel, Elias. Dau: Sarah WILSON (wife/ George). Family Burying Ground. Land: Joseph CONWELL, Joseph H. SMITH, John WILSON, David HAZZARD, James M. CARY, Thomas DRAPER. Wit: Nehemiah DORMAN, John C. HAZZARD. Bond: Capt. Thomas ROBINSON.

pg 489

WEST, Reuben   7JAN1859   24MAR1859
Wife: Nancy (EX). Sons: George E. & Charles H. (both U21). Daus: Rebecca W., Martha Ann, Elizabeth C. & Clara Ella (all U21). Wit: Gideon W. LYNCH, Mary A. LYNCH, Peleg W. HELM.
Bond: Henry R. JOHNSON.

pg 492

LYNCH, John L.   Little Cr H.   10DEC1858   21JUN1859
Wife: Hetty (EX). Sons: James H. (EX), William R., John L., Samuel N., Edgus (youngest). Daus: Mary E., Julia Jane, Sarah Adeline, Amanda P., Ann Eliza. Land: William SIRMAN, John JAMES (dec), Nutter GORDY, Eliza GORDY, Broad Creek H., William HITCH, Samuel D. VAUGHAN, Sarah A. PAYNTER. Wit: B.W. CALLAWAY, W.B. RECORDS.

pg 495

NEWTON, Benjamin   Dags. H.   16JUN1859   25JUN1859
Wife: Elizabeth. Men: Hester Ann CANNON, Caroline V.P.OTWELL, John Lewes SHORT. EX- Dr. John MARTIN. Wit: Hiram S. SHORT, John SHORT, John MARTIN.

pg 497

MESSICK, William   Broadkiln H.   11JUN1859   20JUL1859
Wife: Betsey. Sons: Kendal D., George. Dau: Mary Ann CARPENTER. EX- John MACKLIN (son/ I.). Wit: Robert B. WORKMAN, John MACKLIN (son/ I.). Bond: William F. JONES.

pg 498

KING, Southy   26NOV1847   7SEP1859
Wife: Lizabeth. Sons: Nathaniel, Noble J., Benjamin S., Joshua C. Daus: Levinia, Mary, Leuarana. Wit: Silas J. PENAWELL, Lemuel PENAWELL.

pg 500

MARSH, Jane   Lewes & Rehoboth H.   18AUG1859   7SEP1859
Sis: Mary M. COOPER. Men: James MARSH, Sarah THOMPSON (wife/ John M.), Louisa ROBERTS. Wit: Thomas WALKER, Dr. David HALL. EX- George M. COOPER.

pg 502

BURTON, William N.   Ind Riv H.   22AUG1859   26SEP1859
Wife: Priscilla (EX). Wit: Thomas W. BURTON, Peter R. BURTON.

pg 503

SIRMAN, Ebby   6JUN1859   19NOV1859
Sis: Mary KINNEY. Nieces: Sarah Ann WEST, Sarah Catherine SIRMAN, Amelia Jane KINNEY, Mary Hester SIRMAN. Wit: Winder HEARN, Levin J. HILL. EX- Elijah HITCH.

SMITH, William   Little Creek H.   26OCT1859   29OCT1859
Wife: Levinia (EX). Sons: John Thomas (U21), William Irving (U21), George Richard, Uriah Benjamin. Dau: Mary Catherine. EX- Marshall SMITH & Joseph HEARN. Wit: Joseph HEARN, Asa J. TURPIN, Isaac G. HEARN. Bond: Joseph D. SMITH.

MARVEL, Sally   Dags. H.   6JUN1855   16DEC1859
Son: David. Dau: Elizabeth ENNIS. Grdaus: Mettymere A. ENNIS, Louisa A. SHORT, Maranda L. DONOHO, Elizabeth J. JOHNSON. Great-grdaus: Catherine DONOHO, Margaret DONOHO, Elizabeth P. ENNIS. Men: Sarah A. LYNCH (dau/ Greensbury). EX- Nutter MARVEL. Wit: Aaron B. MARVEL, Louisa H. SHORT.

JOHNSON, Elisha   4FEB1857   21DEC1859
Wife: Eliza. Sons: William D., Alexander, Josiah M., Purnell. Dau: Sarah Eliza. Men: Sarah Ann SCOTT (dau/ wife). EX- Purnel TATMAN. Wit: William H. RICHARDSON, W.W. STEWART. Mary Jane SCOTT (now GIESEN), Nathaniel SCOTT.

HUDSON, Lemuel Sr.   Baltimore H.   2AUG1859   5JAN1860
Wife: unnamed. Sons: Peter R., Benjamin, Noah. Daus: Jane HOLLOWAY (wife/ Peter). Elizabeth, Nancy HUDSON (wife/ Robert, son/ Seth), Catherine. Grsons: John Henry HUDSON (U21, son/ Benjamin), Armwell HOLLOWAY (U21, son/ Peter). EX- John T. LONG/ Frankford. Wit: John HICKMAN, Henry W. LONG, Luther W. CANNON.

WAPLES, Sarah   Milton   9DEC1857   24FEB1860
Son: Gideon B. (EX). Daus: Hetty Ann PRIMROSS (wife/ John), Sarah W. PONDER (wife/ James). Son-law: James PONDER (EX). Wit: John PONDER, J.H. TERRY.

INDEX

27

BURTON, David	10,12*	CAMPBELL, Elizabeth	3	CARY, Nehemiah	9*
BURTON, Edward	13,23	CAMPBELL, John	3*,6	CARY, Rebecca	14
BURTON, Frances	22	CAMPBELL, Mary	3	CHAMBERS, George	5
BURTON, Gideon	22	CAMPBELL, Robert	3	CHIPMAN, William	4
BURTON, Henry	17	CAMPBELL, Susan	3	CLARK, Adam	12
BURTON, Isaac	18,22	CAMPBELL, William	18	CLAY, Jehu	6
BURTON, Jacob	23	CANNON, Barthallomew	12	CLENDANIEL, Benjamin	1
BURTON, James	4,9,13	CANNON, Charles	12	CLENDANIEL, Gemima	1
	17,20,23	CANNON, Clement	19	CLENDANIEL, George	1*
BURTON, Jane	22	CANNON, Cornelius	20	CLENDANIEL, John	1
BURTON, John	6,10,12	CANNON, Daniel	1,20,21	CLENDANIEL, Sally	1
	17,20,22	CANNON, Elijah	11	CLENDANIEL, Samuel	1
BURTON, Lemuel	23	CANNON, Elizabeth	6	CLENDANIEL, Sarah	1
BURTON, Lydia	23	CANNON, George	12,24	CLIFTON, Asa	19
BURTON, Mary	10	CANNON, Hester	12,25	CLIFTON, Catherine	10*
BURTON, Nathaniel	3	CANNON, James	6,12	CLIFTON, Elizabeth	10,19
BURTON, Peter	8,10,12	CANNON, John	12*	CLIFTON, James	19
	25	CANNON, Louder	1	CLIFTON, John	19
BURTON, Polly	17*	CANNON, Luther	26	CLIFTON, Levica	19*
BURTON, Priscilla	25	CANNON, Margaret	15	CLIFTON, Louisa	10
BURTON, Robert	9,13*	CANNON, Mary	12	CLIFTON, Nathan	13
BURTON, Samuel	10	CANNON, Matilda	14	CLIFTON, Pemberton	10,19
BURTON, Sarah	13,17	CANNON, Nutter	17	COBB, Isaac	7
BURTON, T.W.	1	CANNON, Rachel	15*	COFFIN, Arcada	2
BURTON, Thomas	25	CANNON, Stansbury	12	COFFIN, Jacob	16
BURTON, Virginia	12	CANNON, William	6,12,18	COFFIN, James	2,3,6
BURTON, William	23,25*	CAREY, Elisha	13*	COFFIN, Robert	16
BUTLER, Elizabeth	10	CAREY, Hester	13	COLBORN, Sarah	23
BUTLER, James	10	CAREY, James	13	COLEMAN, James	23
BYERS, Joseph	11	CAREY, John	18	COLLINS, Ann	12,24
C		CAREY, Jonathan	17	COLLINS, Charlotte	17
CADE, Ann	12	CAREY, Joseph	16	COLLINS, Doughty	1
CADE, Nancy	19	CAREY, Margaret	16	COLLINS, Edward	12
CALHENE, Peter	15	CAREY, Mary	13	COLLINS, Eli	11
CALHERN, George	23	CAREY, Nancy	18	COLLINS, Elisha	17
CALHERN, Peter	16	CAREY, Peter	18*	COLLINS, Elizabeth	12*,24
CALHERN, Thomas	22.24	CAREY, Stephen	18	COLLINS, Francis	12
CALHOUN, Alexander	17	CAREY, William	13	COLLINS, George	11*,12,18
CALHOUN, David	17	CARLENE, Willmena	3	COLLINS, Georgia	5
CALHOUN, George	17	CARLISLE, Elizabeth	22	COLLINS, Isaac	9
CALHOUN, Madalene	17	CARLISLE, Manlove	8	COLLINS, Isadorah	5
CALHOUN, Missouri	17	CARLISLE, Thomas	22	COLLINS, James	19
CALHOUN, Sidney	17	CARLISLE, William	22	COLLINS, John	11
CALHOUN, Thomas	17	CARPENTER, Eliza	22	COLLINS, Joseph	12,24
CALHOUN, William	17	CARPENTER, Elizabeth	16	COLLINS, Julia	5
CALLAWAY, B.W.	25	CARPENTER, Isaac	13	COLLINS, Levin	5*
CALLAWAY, Ebenezer	24*	CARPENTER, Jane	17	COLLINS, Maria	12
CALLAWAY, Elihu	24	CARPENTER, Mary	25	COLLINS, Marie	24
CALLAWAY, Elijah	15*	CARPENTER, Sally	4	COLLINS, Martha	12,24
CALLAWAY, Elizabeth	15	CARPENTER, Thomas	7,23	COLLINS, Mary	9,12
CALLAWAY, Harry	24	CARY, Albert	2		23,24
CALLAWAY, Isaac	24	CARY, Cornelius	9		
CALLAWAY, John	24	CARY, Eli	9	COLLINS, Samuel	12
CALLAWAY, Mary	24	CARY, Hester	2	COLLINS, Theophelus	12
CALLAWAY, William	15,24	CARY, James	25	COLLINS, Theophilus	14,22
CAMPBELL, Catherine	3	CARY, John	4	COLLINS, William	11
CAMPBELL, Charlotte	3,6	CARY, Lydia	4	COLLISON, Rebecca	1
				COLLISON, William	1

COLUSTER, Milly	20	CULVER, Hardy	24	DAVIS, Solomon	6
COLUSTER, Peter	20	CURRY, Daniel	24	DAVIS, Thomas	10*,16,24
CONAWAY, Elizabeth	5	**D**		DAVIS, William	2*,6
CONAWAY, William	5	DAISEY, James	8	DAWSON, Bayard	12*
CONNALLY, Charles	17	DALE, Charles	8	DAWSON, Joseph	20
CONNAWAY, Betsey	17	DALE, Eli	8*	DAWSON, Prudence	3*
CONNAWAY, Curtis	2,24	DALE, James	8	DAWSON, Sally	20
CONNAWAY, Elizabeth	3	DALE, Jesse	8	DAWSON, Sarah	3
CONNAWAY, James	17	DALE, John	8	DAY, Hester	24
CONNAWAY, John	6,17	DALE, Josiah	8	DAY, John	13,22
CONNAWAY, Mary	16	DALE, Rhoda	8	DAZEY, Hester	24
CONNAWAY, Minos	2,24	DANIEL, Abraham	8	DAZEY, Jacob	5
CONNAWAY, Mires	17	DANIEL, Clement	10	DAZEY, Matilda	5*
CONNAWAY, Nancy	3	DARBE, Nancy	6	DAZEY, Richard	5
CONNAWAY, Nathaniel	17	DARBY, Elexander	6	DAZEY, Susan	5
CONNAWAY, Noble	6,17	DARBY, Nancy	6	DAZEY, Walter	5
CONNAWAY, Sally	6	DARTER, Gilly	9	DENNIS, Benjamin	23
CONNAWAY, Selby	2	DARTER, Hiram	9	DENNIS, Mary	23
CONWELL, Ann	14	DARTER, James	9	DEPUTY, James	13
CONWELL, Asa	11	DARTER, Randolph	9	DEPUTY, Joshua	13
CONWELL, Joseph	16,25	DARTER, Sally	9*	DEPUTY, Rachel	23*
CONWELL, William	16	DARTER, Samuel	9	DEPUTY, Sarah	13
COOPER, David	2	DARTER, Whitefield	9	DEPUTY, Sylvester	13
COOPER, George	25	DASHELL, William	12,18	DEPUTY, Zacheriah	13*
COOPER, James	18	DASHIELL, W.W.	20	DERECKSON, Jehu	10
COOPER, Mary	25	DASHIELL, Winder	5	DERECKSON, Jehu	13
CORDREY, Hessy	1	DASHIELLS, William	5	DERICKSON, Dagworthy	20,23
CORDREY, Spencer	1*	DAVIDSON, Charlotte	9	DERICKSON, Harbinson	14
CORDREY, William	1	DAVIDSON, Cornelius	16	DERICKSON, James	14
CORDRY, Aren	16	DAVIDSON, James	9*	DERICKSON, Jane	24
CORDRY, Betsey	16	DAVIDSON, John	9	DERICKSON, Jehu	6,14,21
CORDRY, John	16	DAVIDSON, Lemuel	9,10,11	DERICKSON, Job	14
CORDRY, Josiah	16*		19	DERICKSON, John	6
CORDRY, Nancy	16	DAVIDSON, Mary	9	DERICKSON, Levin	14
CORDRY, William	16	DAVIDSON, Nathan	9	DERICKSON, Mary	6,14*
COTTINGHAM, Alfred	5,8	DAVIDSON, Samuel	9,22	DERICKSON, Matilda	21
COTTINGHAM, Lavinia	5,8	DAVIS, Brinkley	6*	DERICKSON, Nathaniel	6,21
COULTER, Cornelius	13,16*	DAVIS, Caroline	6	DERICKSON, Sarah	14
COULTER, Eliza	16	DAVIS, Charles	2	DICKERSON, Catherine	18
COULTER, Hetty	16	DAVIS, Dennard	14	DICKERSON, Elizabeth	14
COULTER, John	16	DAVIS, Eli	8	DICKERSON, Jacob	14
COULTER, Joseph	16	DAVIS, Elisha	8	DICKERSON, James	19*
COULTER, Joshua	16	DAVIS, Elizabeth	14,24	DICKERSON, Jonathan	3
COULTER, Mary	16	DAVIS, George	15,22	DICKERSON, Mary	19
COULTER, Sarah	16	DAVIS, Henry	6,10,24	DICKERSON, Miles	13
COULTER, Thomas	16	DAVIS, Hester	6,10	DICKERSON, Nancy	19
COULTER, William	16	DAVIS, Hetty	7	DICKERSON, Peter	14
COVERDALE, Elias	18	DAVIS, John	6,13,20	DICKERSON, Samuel	19
COVERDALE, Levin	22		24	DICKERSON, Sarah	14*
COY, Hugh	3	DAVIS, Joshua	6	DIRECKSON, James	7*
CRAIG, James	22	DAVIS, Lot	24	DIRECKSON, Lemuel	7
CRAIG, Robert	22*	DAVIS, Mark	24	DIRECKSON, Mary	7
CRAIG, Samuel	21	DAVIS, Matthew	14	DIRICKSON, Benjamin	13
CRAIG, William	21	DAVIS, Nehemiah	6,24*	DIRICKSON, Hetty	13
CUBBAGE, Luisa	4	DAVIS, Patty	14	DIRICKSON, Joseph	13
CUBBAGE, Samuel	4	DAVIS, Robert	10	DIRICKSON, Levin	13*
CULLEN, Charles	17,21	DAVIS, Sarah	24	DIRICKSON, Matilda	13

DIRICKSON, Peter	13	**E**			EVANS, Edward	24	
DODD, Hester	9	EDGIN, Jane	4		EVANS, Elijah	6	
DODD, Joseph	8	EDGIN, Mary	4*		EVANS, Eliza	13	
DODD, William	17	EDGIN, Milley	4		EVANS, Enoch	10	
DONOHO, Catherine	26	EDGIN, Millie	4		EVANS, Henry	3,13	
DONOHO, Maranda	26	EDGIN, Robert	4		EVANS, Hetty	24	
DONOHO, Margaret	26	EDGIN, William	4		EVANS, Isaac	24*	
DONOVAN, Abraham	2	EDINGTON, John	21		EVANS, Jacob	3	
DONOVAN, Eli	16	EDINGTON, Mary	16,21		EVANS, James	13	
DONOVAN, Eliza	23	EDINGTON, Sarah	21		EVANS, John	3,24	
DONOVAN, James	16,23*	EDINGTON, William	21*		EVANS, Joshua	8,13,24	
DONOVAN, Kendal	2	EKRIDGE, Susanna	19		EVANS, N.W.	3,13	
DONOVAN, Mary	2*	ELENSWORTH, George	22		EVANS, Nancy	3	
DONOVAN, Nancy	16,23	ELENSWORTH, William	22		EVANS, Rhoda	3	
DONOVAN, Sarah	16	ELLEGOOD, John	14,19		EVANS, Stephen	10	
DONOVAN, William	13,23	ELLEGOOD, Peggy	4		EVANS, William	3,13	
DONOVAN, Wingate	16*	ELLEGOOD, Robert	17		EVANS, Zadoc	3*	
DORMAN, Nehemiah	25	ELLEGOOD, William	17,18		EWING, Adolphus	2	
DOUGLASS, Henry	11		21,24		**F**		
DOWNING, Margaret	21	ELLENWORTH, David	20		FISHER, Alexander	2	
DRAIN, Albert	19	ELLENSWORTH, Nancy	20		FISHER, Catherine	24	
DRAIN, George	19	ELLINGSWORTH, Luke	8		FISHER, Daniel	24	
DRAIN, Lorenzo	19	ELLINGSWORTH, Noble	16		FISHER, Elisa	22	
DRAIN, Sally	19	ELLIOTT, Adaline	17		FISHER, Eliza	16,21	
DRAIN, Sheperd	19*	ELLIOTT, Andrew	7		FISHER, Frank	24	
DRAIN, Shepherd	19	ELLIOTT, George	7		FISHER, George	5,10,12	
DRAIN, Stanford	19	ELLIOTT, Henry	24		FISHER, James	24*	
DRAPER, Elizabeth	6	ELLIOTT, James	7		FISHER, John	16,21	
DRAPER, Henry	6	ELLIOTT, John	17		FISHER, Luther	24	
DRAPER, James	6	ELLIOTT, Joseph	17*		FISHER, Maria	2	
DRAPER, Josephine	6	ELLIOTT, Louisa	11		FISHER, Mary	21,24	
DRAPER, Miers	6	ELLIOTT, Margaret	7*		FISHER, Sally	16	
DRAPER, Myres	24	ELLIOTT, Margarett	14		FISHER, Thomas	10	
DRAPER, Rachel	24	ELLIOTT, Mary	7,14		FISHER, William	16	
DRAPER, Radcliff	24	ELLIOTT, Meshack	1,14*		FLEETWOOD, Cyrus	6	
DRAPER, Sarah	24	ELLIOTT, Sarah	7		FLEETWOOD, Tabitha	17	
DRAPER, Thomas	6*,25	ELLIOTT, Wingate	17		FLEETWOOD, William	17	
DUFFEL, James	23	ELLIS, Elizabeth	1		FOOKS, Ann	16	
DUFFEL, Thomas	23	ELLIS, George	13,15		FOOKS, Benjamin	16*	
DUKES, John	10,17	ELLIS, Isaiah	3		FOOKS, Charles	16	
DUKES, Mary	10	ELLIS, James	13,24		FOOKS, Cyrus	3	
DUKES, Paynter	10	ELLIS, Mary	13		FOOKS, Daniel	16	
DUKES, Thomas	10	ELLIS, Robert	15		FOOKS, Elizabeth	16	
DULANEY, William	2	ELLIS, William	13		FOOKS, George	19	
DULANY, James	1	ELZEY, Alfred	1,13		FOOKS, Henry	16	
DULANY, Levin	1*	ELZEY, Arnold	1		FOOKS, Hetty	20	
DULANY, Martha	1	ELZEY, Charles	1		FOOKS, Isaac	5,8,24	
DULANY, Mary	1	ELZEY, Mary	1,13*		FOOKS, John	16	
DULANY, William	1	ELZEY, Robert	1*,13		FOOKS, Jonathan	10	
DUNNING, Clara	16	ENNIS, Elizabeth	26		FOOKS, Kendal	16	
DUNNING, Elizabeth	16	ENNIS, Jesse	9		FOOKS, Mary	16,21	
DUNNING, Henry	16	ENNIS, Joseph	19		FOOKS, Priscilla	5,8	
DUNNING, John	16	ENNIS, Mettymere	26		FOOKS, Sally	5,8*	
DUNNING, William	16	ENNIS, Sarah	9		FOOKS, Sarah	16	
DURHAM, John	13	EVANS, Catherine	24		FOOKS, Thomas	5*,8,20	
DURHAM, Richard	13	EVANS, Clement	3		FOUNTAIN, Copes	10	
DUTTON, Elizabeth	3	EVANS, Curtis	24		FOWLER, William'	5	

Name	Ref.	Name	Ref.	Name	Ref.
FRAME, George	3	GROVES, Elzey	10		16,20
FRAMPTON, Leatitia	15	GRUNDY, John	13	HEARN, Benjamin	15,23
FRAMPTON, Solomon	11	GUM, Manaen	17	HEARN, Daniel	14
FREENY, William	8	GUNBY, Jacob	4	HEARN, Hiram	7
FRISH, Margaret	19	GUNBY, John	22	HEARN, Isaac	26
FURMAN, Amanda	11	**H**		HEARN, John	21
FURMAN, Edward	11	HALE, William	3	HEARN, Jonathan	17,21
FURMAN, Gatty	11	HALL, Charles	10,21	HEARN, Joseph	26
FURMAN, George	11	HALL, David	25	HEARN, Margaret	3
FURMAN, Hetty	11	HALL, George	13,21	HEARN, Mary	9
FURMAN, James	11	HALL, H.F.	5	HEARN, Nehemiah	9
FURMAN, Jehu	11*	HALL, Henry	3,7	HEARN, Phebe	23
FURMAN, Laura	11	HALL, Jincy	13,23	HEARN, William	9
FURMAN, Lousenda	11	HALL, John	10	HEARN, Winder	25
FURMAN, Martha	11	HALL, Joseph	7,10,24	HEAVELOE, Sarah	18*
FURNIS, Littleton	17	HALL, Lemuel	10*	HELLEN, George	22
G		HALL, Milly	21	HELM, Peleg	6,11,15
GERMAN, John	23	HALL, Philip	10,21		25
GERMAN, Sally	23	HALL, Robert	3,16,23	HEMMONS, David	22
GIESEN, Mary	26	HALL, Sarah	10,21*	HEMMONS, James	22
GILES, Isaac	12	HALL, Thomas	10,21	HEMMONS, John	22
GILES, William	22	HALL, William	7,10,14	HEMMONS, Joshua	22
GODWINE, David	10,21		24	HEMMONS, Peggy	22
GORDEN, David	7*	HAMILL, Hugh	17	HEMMONS, William	22*
GORDEN, Frances	7	HAMMOND, L.P.	9	HENRY, C.W.	1
GORDEN, James	7	HAMMOND, Martha	10	HENRY, George	23
GORDY, Aren	18	HAMMOND, William	10	HENRY, Jane	1
GORDY, Eliza	25	HANDREACK Mary	3	HENRY, John	19
GORDY, John	12*,14	HANDREACK, Kendal	3	HENRY, Luther	1
GORDY, Louisa	18	HARRIS, George	20,24	HENRY, Martha	19
GORDY, Mary	12	HARRIS, Mary	2	HENRY, Mary	1
GORDY, Nutter	25	HARRIS, N.P.	19	HENRY, Sarah	19*
GORDY, Seth	12	HARRIS, Nathaniel	3	HENRY, Stephen	19
GORDY, Thomas	12	HARRIS, William	7	HENRY, William	19
GOSLEE, Hetty	16	HART, Cornelius	16	HICKMAN, Caleb	23
GOSLEE, Samuel	16	HASTING, Archelaus	10	HICKMAN, Charles	15
GOSLEN, Ann	2	HASTING, David	16	HICKMAN, Elizabeth	14
GOSLEN, Hester	2*	HASTING, Grace	16	HICKMAN, Henry	11,21
GOSLEN, Mary	2	HASTING, Lemuel	21	HICKMAN, Hetty	11
GOSLEN, Sarah	2	HASTING, William	10	HICKMAN, Jacob	7
GOSLIN, John	20	HAZZARD, Ann	20	HICKMAN, James	8
GRAY, Emeline	6	HAZZARD, Arthur	14,20*	HICKMAN, John	3,23,26
GRAY, Johnson	8	HAZZARD, David	11,13,16	HICKMAN, Louisa	17
GREEN, Arcada	9		20,25	HICKMAN, Lyddy	11
GREEN, Benjamin	9	HAZZARD, Eliza	21	HICKMAN, Martine	8
GREEN, Eliza	9	HAZZARD, Esther	21	HICKMAN, Mary	14,23
GREEN, George	9	HAZZARD, Georgeanna	12	HICKMAN, Nathaniel	12,15
GREEN, John	9*	HAZZARD, John	3,9,13,14	HICKMAN, Rachel	23
GREEN, Leah	9		15,17,20	HICKMAN, Sarah	17,23
GREEN, Lydia	9		21*,23,25	HICKMAN, Tabitha	14
GREEN, Stephen	1,13	HAZZARD, Joseph	20	HICKMAN, William	15,17*
GREEN, Susan	9	HAZZARD, Mary	20,21		23*
GREEN, William	9	HAZZARD, Richard	20	HIGGINS, Anthony	17
GRIER, Mark	24	HAZZARD, Roads	18	HIGMAN, Daniel	15
GRIFFITH, Joshua	10	HAZZARD, Robert	14,20	HIGMAN, John	15*
GRIFFITH, Mary	15*,16	HAZZARD, Thomas	20	HIGMAN, Priscilla	15
GRIFFITH, Robert	16	HAZZARD, William	2,12,13	HIGMAN, Richard	15

HIGMAN, Robert	15	HOUSTON, John	16,23*	INGRAM, John	6	
HILL, Elizabeth	21*	HOUSTON, July	23	INGRAM, Elizabeth	6	
HILL, Henry	7	HOUSTON, Martin	23	INSLEY, Rebecca	21	
HILL, Levin	25	HOUSTON, Robert	5,16,20	IRVING, Levin	15	
HILL, Lydia	21		23	ISAACS, Minos	17	
HILL, Mary	22	HOUSTON, S.P.	23	ISAACS, Seny	17	
HILL, Polly	7	HOUSTON, Thomas	23	**J**		
HILL, William	22	HOUSTON, William	23	JACKSON, James	8	
HILL, Zadoc	7*	HOUSTON, Zilby	23	JACKSON, Julius	8,23	
HITCH, Elijah	8,25	HOW, James	17*	JACKSON, Peter	22	
HITCH, Henry	8	HOW, John	17	JACKSON, Pinkston	23	
HITCH, Levin	16	HOW, Latitia	17	JACKSON, William	8	
HITCH, Nelly	15	HOWARD, Eliza	10	JACOBS, Curtis	6,19	
HITCH, Samuel	16	HOWARD, Margaret	10	JACOBS, Elizabeth	6	
HITCH, William	10,14,25	HOWARD, Richard	10	JACOBS, Henrietta	19	
HOBBS, George	6	HOWARD, Robert	10	JACOBS, John	19	
HOBBS, Mary	6*	HOWARD, Thomas	7,10*	JACOBS, Luther	19	
HOLLAND, Andrew	16	HUDSON, Aaron	21	JACOBS, Mary	6	
HOLLAND, Betsey	16	HUDSON, Benjamin	6,12,21*	JACOBS, Minos	6	
HOLLAND, Comfort	15,17		26	JACOBS, Noah	6	
HOLLAND, DAVID	3	HUDSON, Catherine	26	JACOBS, Robert	6	
HOLLAND, Elijah	5*	HUDSON, Clement	1	JACOBS, Romelus	19	
HOLLAND, Elisha	12	HUDSON, David	21	JACOBS, Rufus	19	
HOLLAND, Louise	12	HUDSON, Edward	8	JACOBS, Sarah	20	
HOLLAND, Mary	5	HUDSON, Eleanor	8	JACOBS, Stansbury	19*	
HOLLAND, Peter	15,17*	HUDSON, Elijah	10	JACOBS, Starlina	6	
HOLLAND, William	24	HUDSON, Elizabeth	17,21,26	JACOBS, Thomas	5,11,15	
HOLLOWAY, Armwell	26	HUDSON, Henry	5,8,18		20	
HOLLOWAY, Jacob	14	HUDSON, Hetty	21	JACOBS, Timothy	6*	
HOLLOWAY, Jane	26	HUDSON, James	8	JACOBS, William	12,19	
HOLLOWAY, Peter	26	HUDSON, Jeremiah	18	JAMES, Branson	2	
HOLLOWAY, Sarah	14	HUDSON, John	3,6,26	JAMES, Caldwell	2*	
HOLT, Mary	21	HUDSON, Lemuel	26*	JAMES, Catherine	24	
HOLT, Miles	21	HUDSON, Lydia	8	JAMES, Coldwell	24	
HOLT, William	21*	HUDSON, Margaret	18	JAMES, Cornelius	24	
HOOD, Hester	9	HUDSON, Mary	3,18,21	JAMES, Eliza	6	
HOOD, James	9	HUDSON, Nancy	26	JAMES, Erais	2	
HOOD, John	5,8,10	HUDSON, Nathaniel	17	JAMES, Hiram	5,8,24	
HOOPER, Mary	23	HUDSON, Noah	26	JAMES, John	2,25	
HOPKINS, Isaac	8	HUDSON, Peter	26	JAMES, Joshua	24	
HOPKINS, James	9	HUDSON, Polly	21	JAMES, Leah	8	
HOPKINS, Levin	10,15	HUDSON, Robert	26	JAMES, Lucinda	8	
HOPKINS, Mary	8	HUDSON, Seth	26	JAMES, Mary	2,5,8,24	
HOPKINS, Nancy	8	HUDSON, Thomas	8	JAMES, Nancy	24	
HOPKINS, Peter	19	HUDSON, William	22	JAMES, Noah	2,24	
HOPKINS, Sally	8	HUFFINGTON, Rachel	22*	JAMES, Robert	8,24*	
HOPKINS, William	17	HUNTER, Albert	2	JAMES, Rubin	24	
HORSEY, George	12,16	HUNTER, Maria	2	JAMES, Sarah	8	
HORSEY, Nathaniel	1,2,5	HURDLE, Eliza	7	JAMES, Urias	6	
	11,24	HURDLE, Jacob	7*	JAMES, William	2	
HOSKINS, James	15	HURDLE, Joseph	7,19,22	JEARMAN, Isaac	11	
HOUSTON, David	12,16	HURDLE, William	7	JEFFERSON, Ann	15	
HOUSTON, Elisha	23	HURT, Samuel	13	JEFFERSON, Robert	3	
HOUSTON, Eliza	23	HURT, Susan	6	JEFFERSON, Samuel	15	
HOUSTON, Elizabeth	16*	HUSTON, Elisha	11	JEFFERSON, W.E.	24	
HOUSTON, Isaac	20	HUSTON, Zipporah	11	JEFFERSON, Walter	5,18	
HOUSTON, James	19,23	**I**		JEFFERSON, William	10,19	

LINGO, Frances	7	LYNCH, Greensbury	26	MARVELL. Collins	9
LINGO, Hammon	7	LYNCH, Hetty	25	MARVIL. Elizabeth	17*
LINGO, Henry	7*	LYNCH, Isaiah	3	MARVIL. George	17
LINGO, Hetty	1	LYNCH, James	3,16,25	MARVIL. Philip	17
LINGO, Jesse	1*,7	LYNCH, John	25*	MARVILL, Catherine	8
LINGO, John	14*,20	LYNCH, Joshua	11.14	MARVILL. Nathaniel	8
LINGO, Louisa	1	LYNCH, Julia	25	MARVILL. Theodore	8*
LINGO, Mires	1	LYNCH, Lemuel	21	MASON. Charles	16.18
LINGO, Samuel	7	LYNCH, Mary	25	MASSEY, Alexander	10*
LINGO, Sarah	1	LYNCH, Minos	15	MASSEY. Charity	10
LINGO, William	7	LYNCH, Nancy	3	MASSEY, John	10
LODGE, Samuel	23	LYNCH, Rheuban	3	MASSEY. Rina	10
LOFLAND, Alfred	13	LYNCH, Robert	17	MASSEY. Sarah	10
LOFLAND, Cornelius	18	LYNCH, Samuel	25	MATTHEWS. Hezekiah	21
LOFLAND. David	20	LYNCH. Sarah	13,25.26	MAULL. David	22
LOFLAND. Mark	4	LYNCH. William	25	MAULL. Joseph	11
LOFLAND, Samuel	20	LYONS. Laban	20,21,23	MAULL. Mary	11
LONG, Ann	18	**M**		MAULL. Peter	11*
LONG, Benjamin	18	MACKLIN. Elizabeth	21	MAULL. Thomas	23
LONG. Bethshana	18	MACKLIN, John	12,20,25	McCABE. Amos	9,17
LONG, David	4	MACKLIN. Margaret	22	McCABE. Elijah	17
LONG, Delila	18	MACKLIN, Mary	12	McCABE. Elisha	17
LONG, Eliza	18	MALONY. Elizabeth	23	McCABE. Elizabeth	17
LONG. Frankford	26	MANSHIP. Charles	2	McCABE. Garretson	17*
LONG, Henry	26	MARCH. James	23	McCABE. Isaac	17
LONG. Hester	18	MARRINER, Philip	7	McCABE. John	7.17
LONG. Isaiah	18	MARSH, Ann	11	McCABE. Joseph	8
LONG. John	18,26	MARSH, James	25	McCABE. Mary	7
LONG, Joseph	8,18*	MARSH, Jane	25*	McCABE. William	17,18
LONG, Joshua	18	MARSH, Joseph	11	McCALLY. Outen	13
LONG, Mahala	18	MARSH. Mary	21	McCAULLY. Eliza	3
LONG, Mary	18	MARSHALL, Aaron	7,23	McCAULLY. Peter	3
LONG. Nancy	4	MARSHALL. Jane	7	McCOLLY, Betsey	20
LONG, Nathaniel	18	MARSHALL. John	23	McCOLLY. Joshua	20
LONG, Patience	17	MARSHALL. William	7	McCOLLY. Sinia	24
LONG. Rhoda	18	MARTIN, James	9.19	McCOLLY. William	20
LONG, Robert	14	MARTIN. John	2.13,25	McFEE. John	2,20
LONG, Ruth	18	MARTIN, Josiah	16	McFERRAN. Robert	16
LONG. Zeno	17,18	MARTIN, Nancy	16	McGEE. Eliza	9
LOWE, Elizabeth	15	MARTIN. William	16	McGEE. Levin	9
LOWE, George	15	MARVEL, Aaron	10,26	McILVAIN. Benjamin	23
LOWE, James	12	MARVEL, Abraham	22	McILVAIN. Frances	19
LOWE, Ralph	15	MARVEL. Amelia	21	McNEAL. Wilson	8
LOWE. Thomas	4	MARVEL, Catherine	22	MEARS. Thomas	24
LOYD. Catherine	11	MARVEL. Collins	21	MEGEE. Charles	19
LOYD, Elizabeth	13	MARVEL, David	26	MEGEE. David	19
LOYD, Joshua	11	MARVEL, Elizabeth	4	MEGEE. Elon	19
LOYD, Milley	23	MARVEL. George	4	MEGEE. Jane	19
LYNCH, Aaron	3	MARVEL, Josiah	6	MEGEE. John	19
LYNCH, Alfred	3	MARVEL. Manaen	8,11,17	MEGEE. Levin	19
LYNCH, Amanda	25	MARVEL. Mary	21,22	MEGEE. Mary	19
LYNCH, Ann	25	MARVEL, Nancy	3	MEGEE. Moses	9
LYNCH, Edgus	25	MARVEL. Nutter	4,26	MEGEE. Noah	19
LYNCH, Elijah	21	MARVEL. Philip	4*	MEGEE. Patience	19
LYNCH, Elizabeth	3	MARVEL, Sally	26*	MEGEE. Peter	19
LYNCH, Gideon	25	MARVEL. William	22	MEGEE. Rhoda	19
LYNCH, Gilbert	3*	MARVELL. Aaron	17	MEGEE. Thomas	19*

MEGEE, William	19	MOORE, Mary	21*,23	NICHOLS, Hester	20
MELSON, Benjamin	10	MOORE, Nancy	20	NICHOLS, Hetty	23
MELSON, John	5	MOORE, Perry	18	NICHOLS, James	20
MELSON, Josiah	9,17	MOORE, Risdon	16	NICHOLS, Thomas	23
MELSON, Samuel	1	MOORE, Robinson	18	NICHOLSON, Hester	13
MELSON, Sarah	1	MOORE, Sarah	18	NICHOLSON, James	13
MELVIN, John	7	MOORE, Tency	11	NICHOLSON, Levin	15
MELVIN, Margaret	14	MOORE, Thomas	2,5,14	NICHOLSON, Nehemiah	13
MESSICK, Betsey	25		18,23	NOBLE, Alexander	11
MESSICK, Elias	22	MOORE, William	11	NOBLE, Charles	14
MESSICK, Elizabeth	2	MOREAU, Alexander	20	NOBLE, James	13
MESSICK, George	25	MORGAN, Almira	23	NOBLE, Mary	13
MESSICK, Joel	4	MORGAN, James	24	NOBLE, Solomon	11
MESSICK, John	4	MORGAN, Joseph	10	NORMAN, P.B.	8
MESSICK, Julia	8	MORGAN, M.A.	12	NUTTER, Ann	20
MESSICK, Kendal	25	MORGAN, Stephen	12,24	NUTTER, Mary	20
MESSICK, Lydia	22	MORGAN, W.N.	13	**O**	
MESSICK, Minos	17	MORGAN, W.W.	8,9	O'NEAL, Abigal	4
MESSICK, Nathan	4*	MORGAN, Wesley	11,21	O'NEAL, Anthony	4
MESSICK, Salley	4	MORGAN, William	12	O'NEAL, Cyrus	4
MESSICK, Sarah	17	MORINE, Hetty	20	O'NEAL, James	22
MESSICK, Selby	4	MORRIS, Betsey	15	O'NEAL, Josiah	4*
MESSICK, William	2,4,17	MORRIS, David	3	O'NEAL, Margaret	22
	25*	MORRIS, Elias	15	O'NEAL, Pheby	22
MESSICK, Claton	4	MORRIS, George	3,6	O'NEAL, Philip	22
METCALF, John	11,23	MORRIS, James	3	O'NEAL, Pomp	22*
MILBY, Zadoc	17	MORRIS, Jane	9	O'NEAL, Thomas	4
MILLER, James	6	MORRIS, John	9	O'NEAL, William	4
MILMAN, Jonathan	8	MORRIS, Joseph	3,8,9*,10	OBIER, Isaac	24
MITCHELL, Burton	11	MORRIS, Levin	9	OBIER, Jacob	24
MITCHELL, Elijah	11*	MORRIS, Lucy	9	OLIVER, Eleanor	21
MITCHELL, Hetty	11	MORRIS, Michael	9	OLIVER, James	23
MITCHELL, Hyram	11	MORRIS, Rachel	9	OLIVER, Samuel	21
MITCHELL, Isaac	11	MORRIS, Stephen	3*	ORR, William	5,11,15
MITCHELL, James	11	MORRIS, Tabitha	9		16
MITCHELL, Rachel	11	MURRAY, Amy	8	OSBURN, John	17
MITCHELL, Rufus	11	MURRAY, David	7*	OTWELL, Caroline	25
MITCHELL, Saly	11	MURRAY, Joshua	7	OTWELL, Levinia	1
MITCHELL, Samuel	11	MURRAY, Sarah	7	OUTTEN, Daniel	17
MITCHELL, Thomas	4	MURRAY, Stephen	8	OUTTEN, Mary	17
MOORE, Charles	16	MURREY, Laban	8	OWENS, Elijah	19
MOORE, David	18*	MURREY, William	8*	OWENS, James	19
MOORE, E.W.	15,19	MURRY, Joshua	17	OWENS, Jane	19
MOORE, Edward	18	MURRY, Susan	17	OWENS, Jonathan	18
MOORE, Eliza	16	MUSTARD, Cornelius	9,16	OWENS, Mary	4
MOORE, Gaylord	16	**N**		OWENS, Thomas	19*
MOORE, Hester	21	NEAL, Arthur	5,14*	**P**	
MOORE, J.N.	22	NEAL, Charles	14	PALMER, Nancy	22
MOORE, James	19,20*	NEAL, Isaiah	5	PALMER, William	9
MOORE, John	4,15,16	NEAL, James	5,14	PANE, Gove	8
	17,18,19	NEAL, Jonathan	14	PANE, Leah	8
	20,21,23	NEAL, Mary	5	PANE, Lorenzo	8*
MOORE, Jonathan	19	NEAL, Sarah	14	PANE, Mary	8
MOORE, Joseph	21	NEAL, William	5*14	PANE, Thomas	8
MOORE, Julia	21	NENIS, Heaveloe	16	PARKER, Clementine	11
MOORE, Levin	12	NEWTON, Benjamin	25*	PARKER, Edward	11
MOORE, Louisa	23	NEWTON, Elizabeth	25	PARKER, Elizabeth	22*

Name	Ref	Name	Ref	Name	Ref
PARKER, George	11	PHILLIPS, Hosea	12*	PRETTYMAN, James	18,20
PARKER, James	3	PHILLIPS, John	1,10	PRETTYMAN, Josiah	13
PARKER, John	3,11	PHILLIPS, Joseph	10	PRETTYMAN, Levina	10
PARKER, Joseph	11	PHILLIPS, Joshua	1,10,18	PRETTYMAN, Mary	9
PARKER, Mary	11	PHILLIPS, Nancy	10	PRETTYMAN, Paynter	13
PARKER, Peter	3*	PHILLIPS, Naomi	10	PRETTYMAN, Peter	13
PARKER, Samuel	3	PHILLIPS, Nathaniel	1	PRETTYMAN, Purnal	23
PARKER, Theodore	3	PHILLIPS, Noah	1,19	PRETTYMAN, Warren	6
PARKER, William	3	PHILLIPS, Rachel	1	PRETTYMAN, William	4
PARKINSON, Harma	2	PHILLIPS, Sarah	1	PRETTYMAN,Shepard	4*
PARKINSON, Mary	2	PHILLIPS, Shepherd	1	PRIMROSS, Hetty	26
PARSELS, Catherine	15	PHILLIPS, Spencer	1*	PRIMROSS, John	26
PARSELS, Ellen	15	PHILLIPS, Thomas	10*,12	PURNAL, James	10
PARSELS, Ellenor	15	PHILLIPS, William	18	PURNAL, Mary	10
PARSELS, George	15	PHILLIPS,Eunice	1	PUSEY, Andrew	1
PARSONS, James	1	PIERCE, Elizabeth	1	PUSEY, Elihu	14
PARSONS, John	1,15	PIERCE, Henry	10	PUSEY, James	13
PARSONS, Margaret	15	PIERCE, John	1,14	**R**	
PARSONS, Nancy	1	PIERCE, Joshua	14*	RADISH, John	20
PARSONS, Sally	1	PIERCE, Orpha	14	RALPH, Charles	18
PARSONS, Theodore	15	PIERCE, William	14	RALPH, Elizabeth	12
PARSONS, William	1	PLUMMER, Abi	9	RALPH, Mary	18
PARVIS, John	15	PLUMMER, Hudson	9	RALPH, Thomas	13,18*
PARVIS, Mary	15	POLK, Charity	8	RALPH, William	13,18
PAYNTER, Elizabeth	7	POLK, Jes	12	RALPH, William	18
PAYNTER, John	7*	POLK, Josiah	4*	RATCLIFF, Nutter	22
PAYNTER, Joseph	7	POLK, Sarah	4,8	RAWLINS, Charles	22
PAYNTER, Richard	11,17	POLK, Southy	16	RAWLINS, Lot	12,24
PAYNTER, Samuel	7,11,12	POLK, William	4	RAWLINS, P.W.	24
PAYNTER, Sarah	25	PONDER, James	2,16,18	RAWLINS, Philip	12
PENAWELL, Lemuel	25		22,26	RECORDS, Thomas	1,7,24
PENAWELL, Silas	25	PONDER, John	2,7,16	RECORDS, W.B.	20,25
PENNEWELL, George	10		22,26	RECORDS, William	9,18,19
PENNEWELL, Mira	10	PONDER, Sarah	26	REDDEN, James	6,13
PENTON, Elizabeth	11	POOL, Alfred	9	REDDEN, Nehemiah	5
PENTON, James	11*	POOL, Benjamin	9	REED, James	23
PENTON, Mary	11	POOL, Erasmus	9	REYBOLD, Barney	17
PENTON, Mathias	11	POOL, Henry	9	REYNOLDS, Coventon	20*
PENTON, Sarah	11	POOL, Jesse	11	REYNOLDS, David	5,20
PENTON, Susan	11	POOL, John	9	REYNOLDS, George	20
PENTON, William	11,23	POOL, Joshua	9	REYNOLDS, Hester	13
PENUEL, Elisha	9	POOL, Ketturah	9	REYNOLDS, Mary	20
PENUEL, Jane	20*	POOL, Perry	9*	REYNOLDS, Priscilla	2,5*
PENUEL, Josiah	20	POOL, Rebecca	9	REYNOLDS, Roderick	20
PEPPER, A.C.	21	POOL, Robert	9	REYNOLDS, Samuel	13
PETTYJOHN, Mary	18	PORTER, William	4,13,22	REYNOLDS, William	20
PETTYJOHN, Pinkey	18	POTTER, Benjamin	8	REYNOLDS, Zacheriah	20
PETTYJOHN, Pruitt	16	POTTER, Celia	8	RHODES, Elizabeth	23
PHILIPS, George	19	POWELL, Matilda	22	RICHARDS, Charles	18
PHILIPS, William	19	POWELL, Nathaniel	22	RICHARDS, Kendal	21
PHILLIP, John	18	POWELL, William	22	RICHARDS, Mary	14
PHILLIPS, Burton	10	PRATT, Jenetty	4	RICHARDSON, Letitia	20*
PHILLIPS, Elenor	7	PRETTYMAN, Benton	10	RICHARDSON, William	20,26
PHILLIPS, Elihu	1,10,18	PRETTYMAN, Burton	22	RICKARDS Benjamin	9
PHILLIPS, Elizabeth	10,18	PRETTYMAN, Cornelius	3	RICKARDS, Ann	24
PHILLIPS, George	12,17,18	PRETTYMAN, Elizabeth	10	RICKARDS, Charles	13,20
PHILLIPS, Greensbury	1	PRETTYMAN, Isaac	4	RICKARDS, Elias	13

RICKARDS, Eliza	5	ROGERS, John	2,15	SEAVIN, John	2
RICKARDS, Eunice	1	ROGERS, Lambert	15*	SELBY, Josiah	7,8,14
RICKARDS, Isaac	6	ROGERS, Lucinda	15	SELBY, Sampson	9,14
RICKARDS, James	1	ROGERS, Mary	15	SEPPLE, C.B.	6
RICKARDS, John	7,15,24	ROGERS, Thomas	14	SEPPLE, Thomas	13,17,20
RICKARDS, Kendal	6	ROGERS, William	1	SHANKLAND, Mary	11*
RICKARDS, Lemuel	24	ROSS, Caleb	16	SHANKLAND, William	11
RICKARDS, Maria	6	ROSS, Eunice	1,12	SHARP, Asa	5,18
RICKARDS, N.	3	ROSS, Sarah	12*	SHARP, Emely	5*
RICKARDS, Philip	24	ROSS, William	1,19	SHARP, Henry	5,23
RICKARDS, Robert	14	ROUSE, James	3	SHARP, Jacob	5,18
RICKARDS, Sarah	15	ROWLAND, Jacob	23	SHARP, John	5,18
RICKARDS, William	6,10,11	RUSSEL, Alfred	25	SHARP, Joshua	20
RIGGIN, Ann	14	RUSSEL, Betsey	23	SHARP, Kenzey	18
RIGGIN, Matilda	19	RUSSEL, David	25	SHARP, Mary	18*,22
RIGGIN, Robert	14*	RUSSEL, Edward	23	SHARP, Nathaniel	5
RIGGIN, Thomas	14	RUSSEL, Elias	25	SHARP, Sally	8
RIGGIN, William	19	RUSSEL, Essie	23	SHARP, Sarah	1
RILEY, Betsey	4*	RUSSEL, George	25	SHARP, Thomas	8
RILEY,Benjamin	10	RUSSEL, James	15,23	SHAW, William	22
ROACH, Angelina	9	RUSSEL, John	22	SHIPLEY, Joseph	1
ROACH, Elizabeth	15	RUSSEL, Joseph	22	SHIRMAN, John	22
ROACH, Henry	24	RUSSEL, Mary	16,23,25	SHIRMAN, Mary	22
ROACH, Jerusha	24	RUSSEL, R.R.	23	SHIRMAN, Polly	22*
ROACH, John	15	RUSSEL, Robert	23,25*	SHOCKLEY, David	15
ROACH, Mary	15	RUSSEL, Sally	25	SHOCKLEY, Elias	15
ROADS, B.W.	21	RUSSEL, Samual	16,25	SHOCKLEY, John	15
ROBBINS, Ann	14	RUSSEL, William	22*,23*	SHOCKLEY, Lemuel	8,15
ROBBINS, David	14*		25	SHOCKLEY, Matilda	15
ROBBINS, Elizabeth	14	RUST, Absolum	21	SHOCKLEY, Nancy	15
ROBBINS, James	16	RUST, James	9	SHOCKLEY, Wilson	15*
ROBBINS, Jane	16	RUST, Mariah	21	SHOCKLEY,William	15
ROBBINS, John	14	RUST, Peter	16	SHOEMAKER, Jonathan	2,3
ROBBINS, Joseph	5,14	RUST, Thomas	19	SHORT, Alfred	8,24
ROBBINS, Mary	5	RUST, William	21	SHORT, Ann	24
ROBBINS, Mires	14	S		SHORT, Daniel	20,24*
ROBBINS, Sarah	14	SALMON, J.S.	22	SHORT, Elenah	2
ROBERTS, Louisa	25	SALMONS, John	19	SHORT, Eliza	9
ROBINS, David	22	SAMPDEN, Joshua	17	SHORT, Elizabeth	20
ROBINS, Elizabeth	22	SAMPSON, Jenetta	20	SHORT, Gilley	24*
ROBINSON, Benjamin	9	SANDERS, Charles	2	SHORT, Gilly	24
ROBINSON, George	20	SANDERS, Miles	2	SHORT, Hetty	5
ROBINSON, Peter	3	SANFORD, Whiting	16	SHORT, Hiram	11,25
ROBINSON, Thomas	14,19	SATCHEL, James	24	SHORT, John	2,9,24,25
	20,25	SATCHEL, Margaret	24	SHORT, Letty	20
RODNEY, Betsey	5	SATCHEL, Philip	24	SHORT, Louisa	26
RODNEY, Daniel	5*	SATTERFIELD, John	22	SHORT, Nancy	3
RODNEY, Eliza	21	SATTERFIELD, Mary	6	SHORT, Nicholas	17
RODNEY, George	23	SATTERFIELD, Sally	6	SHORT, Purnal	24
RODNEY, J.D.	8,10	SAUNDERS, Thomas	5	SHORT, Samuel	24
RODNEY, John	5,12,21	SCHELLENGER, William	23	SHORT, Solomon	18
RODNEY, Mary	5,21	SCOTT, James	5,12	SHORT, William	9,10,12
RODNEY, Nancy	5	SCOTT, Mary	5,26		24
RODNEY, Robert	5	SCOTT, Naomi	5	SIMPLER, Andrew	16
RODNEY, Sarah	5	SCOTT, Nathaniel	26	SIMPLER, Charles	19
RODNEY, William	5	SCOTT, Purnal	16	SIMPLER, Elizabeth	19
ROGERS, Greensbery	11	SCOTT, Sarah	26	SIMPLER, George	9,19

SIMPLER, Lucy	9			
SIMPLER, Lydia	16	STEEL, John	2,22	
SIMPLER, Sally	16	STEEL, Maria	20	
SIMPSON, William	3	STEEL, Mary	2	
SIRMAN, Ebby	25*	STEEL, Penelope	2,18	
SIRMAN, J.W.	12	STEEL, Sarah	2	
SIRMAN, Mary	25	STEEL, William	2	
SIRMAN, Sarah	25	STEEN, Curtis	5*	
SIRMAN, William	25	STEEN, Ephrain	5	
SLAYTON, Nehemiah	10	STEEN, James	5	
SMALLWOOD, Mary	4	STEEN, Lavenia	5	
SMALLWOOD, Susan	4	STEEN, Levin	5	
SMITH, Alley	15	STEEN, Nancy	5	
SMITH, Bell	20	STEEN, Sarah	5	
SMITH, Betsey	20	STEEN, Thomas	5	
SMITH, Charlton	22	STEEN, William	5	
SMITH, David	10	STEPHENS, Sally	19	
SMITH, Eli	4	STEPHENSON, John	16	
SMITH, Elizabeth	17,24	STEPHENSON, Lydia	16	
SMITH, George	17,26	STEPHENSON, Mary	16	
SMITH, James	16	STEPHENSON, Susan	9	
SMITH, John	1,26	STEPHENSON, Wesley	17	
SMITH, Joseph	2,17*25 26	STEPHENSON, William	16	
		STEWART, W.W.	26	
SMITH, Laurenson	19,20	STOCKLEY, Charles	13	
SMITH, Levinia	26	STOCKLEY, Elon	23	
SMITH, Lydia	17	STOCKLEY, Hannah	13*	
SMITH, Marshall	26	STOCKLEY, Kendal	6	
SMITH, Mary	16,18,26	STOCKLEY, Lemuel	1	
SMITH, Nicholas	24	STOCKLEY, Letty	6	
SMITH, Polly	1	STOCKLY,Gharles	20	
SMITH, Samuel	17	STONE, John	4	
SMITH, Silas	16	STONE, Rachel	4	
SMITH, Uriah	26	STREET, John	12	
SMITH, Wesley	4,12,19	STREET, Patience	2	
SMITH, William	15,,26*	STUART, James	17	
SMULLEN, Comfort	21	STUART, John	2	
SOCKUM, Levin	2	STUART, Mary	2	
SPANISH, Sally	20	STUART, Michael	17	
SPANISH, Seshey	20	STUART, W.W.	1	
SPICER, Curtis	13	STUART, William	17	
SPICER, Dolly	13	SUDLER, John	2	
SPICER, Elzey	13	SUDLER, Joseph	18	
SPICER, Hetty	3	SULLIVAN, Joseph	6	
SPICER, James	3	SULLIVAN, Sarah	6	
SPICER, John	13	SWAIN, Catherine	24	
SPICER, Lewis	24	SWAIN, Cornelius	24	
SPICER, Tilghman	13*	SWAIN, John	20*	
SPICER, William	5,13	SWAIN, Leah	24	
STAFFORD, William	6	SWAIN, Mary	20,24	
STAPLEFORD, Nathaniel	1	SWAIN, Polly	20	
STAPLEFORD, William	1	SWAIN, Priscilla	20	
STEEL, Eliza	2	SWAIN, Sinia	24	
STEEL, Elizabeth	21	SWAIN, Truston	24	
STEEL, George	2	SWAIN, Walter	20	
STEEL, Ishmael	2	SWEENY, Arthur	5	
STEEL, James	2*,5,18	SWEENY, Charles	5	

SWEENY, Edward	5
SWEENY, Elizabeth	5
SWEENY, John	5*
SWEENY, Mary	5
T	
TATMAN, Purnel	26
TATMAN, William	18
TATUM, William	17
TAYLOR, Betsey	5
TAYLOR, Charles	6
TAYLOR, Clarencia	9
TAYLOR, David	5
TAYLOR, Elias	23,24
TAYLOR, Elizabeth	6,24*
TAYLOR, James	6
TAYLOR, John	10,24
TAYLOR, Mary	6,18
TAYLOR, Nancy	6
TEN, Leah	9
TERRY, J.H.	26
THOMAS, Uriah	9
THOMPSON, Augustus	19
THOMPSON, John	25
THOMPSON, Sarah	25
THOROUGHGOOD, Will.	2,6,9
THOROUGHGOOD,Sarah	9
TILNEY, Hannah	13
TILNEY, John	2,13*
TILNEY, Peter	13
TILNEY, Robert	13
TILNEY, William	13
TIMMONS, Esther	14*
TIMMONS, Fanny	14
TIMMONS, Hester	14
TIMMONS, Isaac	14
TIMMONS, James	14
TIMMONS, Lemuel	14
TIMMONS, Stephen	14
TIMMONS, William	4
TINDAL, Ellen	6
TINDAL, John	5,17
TINDLE, Miles	2
TINDLE, Neolden	2
TINKER, D.B.	4,8
TODD, Charles	24
TODD, Clayton	24
TODD, Hetty	24
TODD, Jane	24
TODD, William	24
TONAEUS, Elizabeth	5
TORBERT, Martha	13
TOWNSEND, Allen	2
TOWNSEND, Cutter	2
TOWNSEND, David	1
TOWNSEND, Ebe	15
TOWNSEND, Hannah	25
TOWNSEND, James	1,25

TOWNSEND, John	1	VAUGHAN, Eliza	23	WALTER, Ebe	25
TOWNSEND, Joshua	15	VAUGHAN, Margaret	22	WALTON, Ann	2
TOWNSEND, Kitty	25	VAUGHAN, S.D.	17	WAPLES, Alfred	2
TOWNSEND, Moses	2*	VAUGHAN, Samuel	25	WAPLES, Benton	2
TOWNSEND, Purnal	10	VAUGHAN, William	6	WAPLES, Cornelius	2*,11
TOWNSEND, Rachal	2	VAUGHHAN, Sarah	22	WAPLES, David	2
TOWNSEND, Sally	1	VAUGHN, Joseph	6	WAPLES, George	2
TOWNSEND, Zadoc	25*	VEASEY, Nathaniel	16	WAPLES, Gideon	16,26
TOWNSEND, Zadock	25	VENT, Elizabeth	7	WAPLES, Isaac	1,6*
TREFORD, John	11	VENT, William	7	WAPLES, James	2
TRUITT, Alexander	14	VESSELS, Ann	10	WAPLES, Jane	2
TRUITT, Anderson	9	VESSELS, Charlotte	10	WAPLES, John	2,4,21,22
TRUITT, Benton	18	VESSELS, Hetty	10	WAPLES, Joseph	2
TRUITT, Caleb	9*	VESSELS, Myers	10	WAPLES, Lemuel	16
TRUITT, Catherine	22	VESSELS, Nathaniel	10	WAPLES, Levin	3
TRUITT, David	9	VESSELS, William	10*	WAPLES, Mary	6
TRUITT, Esther	9	VICKERS, Mary	2	WAPLES, Sarah	26*
TRUITT, George	9	VINCENT, George	9,15,22	WAPLES, Sharon	2
TRUITT, Greensberry	18	VINCENT, Noah	2	WAPLES, William	6
TRUITT, James	1	VINSON, Manuel	3	WARD, Cyrus	17
TRUITT, John	1,14	VINSON, Nathaniel	1	WARD, Peggy	4
	18*,22	**W**		WARNER, Louisa	11
TRUITT, Joshua	14	WAINWRIGHT, Jacob	17	WARREN, Alexander	4
TRUITT, Ketturah	9	WAINWRIGHT, John	17	WARREN, Eunice	7*
TRUITT, Lavinia	18	WAINWRIGHT, Mahala	13	WARREN, Isaac	4
TRUITT, Leven	9	WAINWRIGHT, Margaret	9	WARREN, John	4,13
TRUITT, Mary	1,22	WAINWRIGHT, Philip	17*	WARREN, Kendal	13
TRUITT, Philip	3	WALKER, Mary	8	WARREN, Lodawick	7,8
TRUITT, Sarah	18	WALKER, Thomas	5,7,8,	WARREN, Mary	13
TRUITT, Sophia	9		10,21,25	WARREN, Matilda	18
TRUITT, Thomas	11	WALLACE, James	21*	WARREN, Nancy	1,13
TUBBS, Burton	6	WALLACE, Phaney	21	WARREN, Penelope	3
TUBBS, David	23	WALLER, Ebben	7	WARREN, Robert	3,4,13,18
TUNNELL, Elizabeth	13	WALLER, Major	15	WARREN, Samuel	13*,22
TUNNELL, George	13	WALLER, Rachel	15	WARREN, Sarah	13
TUNNELL, James	25	WALLER, William	19	WARREN, Sina	4
TUNNELL, John	10	WALLS, Ann	16	WARREN, Spicer	1
TURNER, Betsey	9	WALLS, Asa	8	WARREN, Stephen	4
TURNER, Charles	2	WALLS, Brinkley	16	WARREN, William	4
TURNER, Daniel	2*	WALLS, David	19	WARRINGTON, Benjamin	9*
TURNER, Elizabeth	25	WALLS, Eliza	3,8	WARRINGTON, Comfort	7
TURNER, Issac	2	WALLS, Emely	3	WARRINGTON, Ebenezer	21
TURNER, James	25	WALLS, Gideon	19	WARRINGTON, Eliza	9
TURNER, Leah	2	WALLS, Izabel	3	WARRINGTON, Elizabeth	4,9
TURNER, Torbert	2	WALLS, James	2,4,7	WARRINGTON, Hetty	16
TURPIN, Asa	26		8,16*	WARRINGTON, James	4*,9
TWILLEY, Emaline	7	WALLS, John	19	WARRINGTON, John	4,9
TWILLEY, James	7	WALLS, Jonathan	3	WARRINGTON, Sarah	4,9
TWILLEY, Joseph	7	WALLS, Margaret	19	WARRINGTON, William	9,15
TWILLEY, Levin	7	WALLS, Mary	19	WATSON, Beniah	10
TWILLEY, Maria	7	WALLS, Nehemiah	19*	WATSON, Bethuel	22
TWILLEY, Mary	7	WALLS, Patience	19	WATSON, Curtis	10,22
TWILLEY, Robert	7*	WALLS, Peter	3,7	WATSON, Daniel	9*
TWILLEY, Julia	7	WALLS, Renattus	19	WATSON, David	8*
V		WALLS, Samuel	16	WATSON, Edward	4
VAUGHAN, Charles	13,18	WALLS, Thomas	7,16	WATSON, Elizabeth	22*
VAUGHAN, Edward	23	WALLS, William	3*,8*,16	WATSON, James	8

WATSON, John	22	WHARTON, John	20*	WILSON, Jonathan	16,23*
WATSON, Joseph	12	WHARTON, Julia	5	WILSON, Kendal	23
WATSON, Mary	22	WHARTON, Martha	20	WILSON, Levin	15
WATSON, Nelly	8	WHARTON, William	24	WILSON, Margaret	16
WATSON, Priscilla	4*	WHEATLEY, William	17	WILSON, Nathanial	23
WATSON, Robert	10	WHEATLY, William	24	WILSON, Sarah	25
WATSON, Sophia	18*	WHITE, Dinah	6	WILSON, Simon	16
WATSON, William	4,10	WHITE, Elizabeth	11	WILSON, Tabitha	22
WEATHERLEY, Betsey	15	WHITE, George	2,14	WILSON, William	3,7,12
WEBB, Jacob	6		18*,22		13,23
WEBB, James	5	WHITE, Purnal	11,12	WILSON, Zacheriah	3
WELCH, Amelia	1	WHITE, Robert	20	WINDOM, John	17
WELCH, George	1,3,15	WHITE, Sophia	18	WINDSOR, C.C.	1,4,12
WELCH, Janney	1	WILKINS, James	15		16,20
WELCH, Joseph	1	WILKINS, Thomas	6	WINDSOR, Cyrus	2,13
WELCH, Luther	1	WILLEN, Isaac	6	WINGATE, Burton	20
WELCH, Lydia	15	WILLEN, Thomas	6	WINGATE, Elijah	20
WELCH, Margaret	1	WILLEY, Edward	24	WINGATE, Hezekiah	20*
WELCH, Mary	3	WILLEY, Elizabeth	24	WINGATE, Isaac	20
WELCH, Nehemiah	3,16,19	WILLEY, George	16	WINGATE, Job	12
	21	WILLEY, John	6,22	WINGATE, John	11,12
WELCH, Peter	3	WILLEY, Joshua	22		18,20
WELCH, Sarah	1	WILLEY, Mary	22	WINGATE, Kendal	2
WELLS, Edward	19	WILLEY, Nehemiah	6*,22	WINGATE, Nancy	20
WELLS, Sally	19	WILLEY, Simeon	22	WINGATE, Stansbery	20
WEST, Charles	25	WILLEY, Susan	6	WOLFE, D.E.	5
WEST, Clara	25	WILLEY, Theodore	22*	WOLFE, D.R.	17
WEST, Elizabeth	15,25	WILLEY, Waitman	20	WOLFE, David	6,16
WEST, George	25	WILLEY, William	20	WOLFE, Dennis	8
WEST, Isaac	10	WILLGEN, Betsey	6	WOLFE, Henry	5,11
WEST, James	3*,21,23	WILLIAMS, Edward	8	WOLFE, James	22
WEST, Jehu	3	WILLIAMS, Eleanor	23	WOLFE, John	8
WEST, Jenet	15	WILLIAMS, Elizabeth	2	WOLFE, Lydia	7,8
WEST, John	3,6,13	WILLIAMS, George	12	WOLFE, Reece	8*
	17,18,21*	WILLIAMS, Hester	14	WOLFE, Rice	7
WEST, Joshua	15*	WILLIAMS, James	14	WOLFE, W.W.	16
WEST, Lavinia	21	WILLIAMS, John	1	WOLFE, William	2,5,6,23
WEST, Lewes	10,23	WILLIAMS, Lavinia	1	WOOTTEN, Isaac	23*
WEST, Mahala	18	WILLIAMS, Lemuel	14	WOOTTEN, Jacob	3,7
WEST, Martha	25	WILLIAMS, Luther	23	WOOTTEN, Nathaniel	23
WEST, Mary	21	WILLIAMS, Nathan	14*	WORKMAN, Philip	16,18
WEST, Nancy	25	WILLIAMS, Serous	9	WORKMAN, Robert	18,25
WEST, Peggy	3	WILLIAMS, William	7,14	WRIGHT, Frettwell	12*
WEST, Peter	15	WILLIS, Fisher	1*	WRIGHT, Gardiner	22
WEST, Priscilla	21	WILSON, Aletta	13	WRIGHT, Gardner	12
WEST, Rachel	15	WILSON, Ann	12,23	WRIGHT, Jacob	22
WEST, Rebecca	25	WILSON, Backley	22	WRIGHT, Lewes	11
WEST, Reuben	25*	WILSON, Barkley	4	WRIGHT, Lewis	14
WEST, Robert	10	WILSON, Charity	23*	WRIGHT, Margret	12
WEST, Ruben	15	WILSON, Charlotte	3	WRIGHT, Mira	13
WEST, Rubin	7	WILSON, David	5,8,12	WRIGHT, Patience	20
WEST, Samuel	21	WILSON, Elias	23	WRIGHT, Peter	12
WEST, Sarah	15,25	WILSON, Elizabeth	5,8,15	WRIGHT, Sina	11
WEST, Thomas	6	WILSON, George	23,25		
WEST, William	3,21	WILSON, Harry	3		
WHALEY, Edward	8	WILSON, James	3*,7,15*		
WHALEY, James	8	WILSON, John	5,12*,25		

www.ingramcontent.com/pod-product-compliance
Lightning Source LLC
Chambersburg PA
CBHW051049030426